Firm

Forward

Edi Osborne

There comes a moment when you have to stop revving up the car and shove it into gear.

David Mahoney

Contact Info:
Edi Osborne, CSPM, Tri-Metrix Certified
Certified Stages of Growth Strategist
CEO, Mentor Plus
P.O. Box 389, Carmel Valley, CA 93924
Ph: 831-659-7587

Library of Congress Control Number: 2013919826
Firm Forward by Edi Osborne, Carmel Valley, CA

Oz Publishing - Printed in the U.S.A.

ISBN-13: 978-1493738335 (Edi Osborne)
ISBN-10: 149373833X

Acknowledgements

I want to thank the members of the Mentor Plus® Consulting Accountants' Round Table who, for over 15 years, have been willing guinea pigs to test out new content and tools and for providing feedback and best practices that helped to shape and improve our curriculum and advisory methodology.

To all my colleagues at MNP: Mark, Jeff, Ted, Kelly, Bob, Lynn, Garth, and the rest of my Canadian "family." Thank you for your commitment to a better way; *the MNP way.*

Thank you to my editors, DJ and Penelope, for all your help in crafting and refining my message. Any undiscovered typos/errors are the fault of the author.

Thank you to my mentor, Jay Abraham, for showing me how to turn my insatiable curiosity into a career asset.

To the Lizards of Oz - you know who you are. Thank you for being the catalyst for this project and all your valuable insight.

Thank you to my parents for giving me the courage to follow my dreams.

I also want to thank my children, Meredith, Stephanie, Charlee, and Ben, for always supporting me and my unconventional approach to life.

The final thank you goes to my husband and business partner, Steve Osborne. Thank you for all the tea, random flowers on my desk (just when I needed a lift), shoulder rubs when my mind was willing and my body wasn't, and encouragement when I was immersed in the creative process. Thank you, also, for being such a great sounding board and collaborator on this and all the efforts that led to the writing of this book.

> *The most important thing in life is not simply to capitalize on your gains. Any fool can do that. The important thing is to profit from your losses. That requires intelligence and makes the difference between a man of sense and a fool.*
>
> *Dale Carnegie*

Contents

*Leadership is the capacity to
translate vision into reality.*

Warren G. Bennis

FOREWORD

Deep down we all want to make a difference. The advisory methodology outlined in this book, has already empowered hundreds of accountants and advisors to make a real difference in their client's businesses. My hope is that this book will help us reach and empower even more. Although the setting for this story is a CPA firm, the principles and methodology can be applied by anyone wanting to become (or expand) their role as a trusted business advisor.

Rapid advances in technology, a global recession, and changing customer expectations have forever altered the rules of business. This new reality demands we up our game if we want to be successful in the future.

Let's just say it out loud: change is hard. However, those who resist change are already learning that maintaining the status quo can be even harder. Those who can embrace the "new normal" are going to find an abundance of opportunities going forward.

A new world of opportunities starts with a fresh perspective. My intent is to present a practical, proven, and sustainable model for delivering high value advisory services. I'll present a blueprint for change that has the potential to revitalize your practice, propel it into the future, empower, engage, and, along the way, maybe even reawaken your passion for the profession. If you are already perfectly content with your practice, this is not the book for you. If you are looking for a roadmap for moving your practice up the value chain – beyond commodity level services – you're in the right place at the right time. Firm Forward is a story you may be all too familiar with: an accounting firm trying to adjust to the changing business environment. You'll shadow the newly appointed Managing Partner, Bennie Stewart, as he takes a non-traditional approach to address three critical issues all firms are grappling with:

1) How to grow the firm?
2) How to attract and retain top talent?
3) How to attract and retain ideal clients?

As the story unfolds, all three of these questions point to one answer: Level 5 Service. What is Level 5 Service?

The short answer: Level 5 Service is a structured approach to providing high value advisory services proven to improve the performance of small businesses. The step-by-step, long answer is what this book is all about.

Level 5 Service changes everything; I see proof of it every day. Accountants and advisors are delivering Level 5 Services and making a real difference in the success of their clients. So much so, business owners have invested over $100 million in Level 5 services.

Level 5 Service may not be right for every practitioner or firm. However, for those who find their sweet spot working side-by-side with their clients to find solutions to their business issues, Level 5 Service will likely be a very good fit for you. Level 5 service is the cure for **Random Acts of Consulting**, those one-off, design-on-the-fly projects offered up in response to a random client need. The Level 5 Service framework is a proactive, systematic, and scalable approach that firms of all sizes can apply to businesses across all industries and niches.

If you're someone who prefers to cut to the chase, then you're probably ready to dive right into the story. Go for it. If you're interested in the back-story behind the evolution of Level 5 Service, keep reading.

The back-story chronicles a process spanning more than

two decades. As I watched it evolve, I witnessed profound results that were nothing less than inspiring. The back-story isn't just the foundation for this book, it's a testament to how far the profession has come and where it is heading in the future. It's also a salute to all the early adopters who suspended their fear of the unknown in pursuit of more meaningful and relevant relationships with their clients.

The Back-Story

I'm not an accountant, but I've presented to thousands of practitioners for over 20 years. I've trained, mentored, and coached hundreds of firm leaders along the way and have tremendous respect for the work they do. I'm grateful for the many opportunities I've had to work with fearless trailblazers and early adopters because they've led me here.

This story is a patchwork of experiences and observations, and while any resemblance to real life is coincidental, don't be surprised if some of the situations strike close to home. They should; that's the point.

I didn't start out working with accountants. My background is small business consulting. In 1989, I started working with marketing guru Jay Abraham. I was blessed with the opportunity to work side-by-side with Jay at his Business Boot Camps and then coach the business owner participants for 12 months as they implemented Jay's business development strategies. The experience I gained from coaching over 100 small businesses in dozens of industries from all over the world laid the foundation for the launch of my own consulting practice.

My practice was performance based: I'd share in the upside of the marketing programs I designed for clients. As I quickly discovered, most small businesses lacked internal performance monitoring systems. If I was going to get paid, I had to roll up my sleeves and dive in. Helping my clients develop performance measurement systems to quantify and better manage performance became a central component of my practice.

Measuring marketing programming effectiveness was just the tip of the iceberg. Once we were generating new leads, I ran into situations where the sales team was ineffective at closing leads. To address this deficiency, I added sales training to my consulting toolkit. Once the sales team was closing more leads (and I was being paid), I ran into situations where operations couldn't keep up with the orders, so I added process improvement to my repertoire. Before long, I was conducting process improvement workshops and developing performance measurement systems across entire organizations.

To be honest, there were times I felt like I was barely a half step ahead of my clients on the learning curve. But over time, pushing myself to learn new skills and study the best practices of successful companies put both my clients and my practice ahead of the game. Today, a simple internet search can yield best practices for just about any issue your clients face. If you're curious enough to ask the question, you'll find the answer or, at a minimum, somebody who knows the answer.

Around the same time, I read *Think and Grow Rich* by Napoleon Hill. I was intrigued by what he called *the mastermind effect*: creating a peer group where members hold each other accountable to their vision. Conducting mastermind-style groups allowed me to leverage my time and talents more effectively and it also came with a profound additional benefit. Positive peer pressure *between* the business owner participants naturally encouraged a greater level of accountability. I also found the format allowed for an invaluable cross-pollination of ideas across industries.

At one time, my partner and I had ten mastermind roundtables throughout California, including group-mentoring sessions through San Jose State University's Women Entrepreneur Program.

In 1991, I was invited to speak to a group of accountants. It was one of those breakfast meetings where CPAs show up for the free food and CPE certificate. We were in the middle of a recession – I remember it like it was yesterday – and I'd been asked to speak about marketing CPA services, but the discussion quickly devolved into a group gripe about the depressed economy and commiserating about clients who weren't paying their bills.

Frankly, the CPAs' unsympathetic attitude toward the plight of their small business clients shocked me. In frustration, I said, "Your focus is all wrong. You need to stop complaining about your clients not paying your bill and start helping them improve cash flow. You'll get paid when they get paid. It's that simple."

I then told this group of CPAs the story of one of Jay Abraham's clients who owned a rock/cement quarry. This owner recognized a very disturbing trend in the industry: contractors jumping from one provider to another when they fell behind on their payables. Homeowners stiffing the contractors begot contractors stiffing vendors, until vendors stopped supplying concrete and the contractors went out of business – a classic lose/lose.

Rather than allowing this trend to take his company down, the owner sent his controller into the field to teach the contractors to cost and bid jobs more accurately, to prepare proposals with larger up-front deposits, to manage change orders, to monitor labor costs, and file mechanic's liens when needed. The controller arranged payment terms with the contractors that allowed them to pay down what was in arrears over time. If they kept up their payments, the owner continued to sell them concrete, as long as they stayed current on all new jobs.

When the other concrete vendors in town refused to work with the contractors who had fallen behind, this owner's out-of-the-box approach kept those struggling contractors in business. They were grateful and fiercely loyal for helping them become smarter operators. As the economy recovered, loyal customers rewarded the owner with all their business, and the "Raving Fan" factor attracted a lot of new business as well.

That breakfast meeting forever altered the direction of my practice. I shifted from helping small businesses directly to training accountants and advisors to perform the kind of performance measurement and management advisory services I was providing.

From that day on, I became a small business advocate to the profession, with the goal of teaching accountants to use their accounting skills beyond finance: to measure critical activities across all areas of business performance. It made perfect sense to me; accountants are *made to measure things.* They are uniquely skilled and positioned to help clients make the connection between day-to-day activities and financial outcomes. The connection starts with a new perspective on profit, something we call The Profit Equation ^{sm}.

To *measure* profit you focus on financial outcomes:
Revenue – Expenses = Profit
Lagging Indicators

If you want to *improve* profit you have to focus on the activities that drive profitability:
People x Process = Profit
Leading Indicators

Being able to make the connection between leading and lagging indicators is fundamental to business success. There was one problem. Most of the CPAs I was running into had limited to no experience running a business; they had gone from school to working in an accounting firm. Their lack of real life business experience and business fundamentals undermined their confidence to expand their offerings beyond traditional services. Making the connection became our mission. We set out to raise the business acumen of accountants, advisors, and the businesses they serve.

To that end, Mentor Plus was born in 1997, and our flagship program, The Mentor Plus® Consulting Accountants' Round Table (a.k.a. CART) was launched. Here we are 15 years later and accountants from across the country still gather three times a year to accomplish four things:

1) Build their acumen and advisory skills with ongoing training,
2) Learn about and adopt new tools and technology,
3) Share best practices and learn from each other, and
4) Gain access to high level mentoring and coaching to remain focused on their goals throughout the year.

We take a 3D approach to every program we offer, focusing on:
1) Mindset,
2) Skill set, and
3) Tool set.

This is important because . . .
1) Tools without the skills to use them are underutilized.
2) Skills without the right mindset are misdirected.
3) Mindset alone, without structured application, results in unleveraged activities.

Without all three dimensions, you end up performing ***Random Acts of Consulting.***

When advisory services are random, practitioners never reach a level of mastery. Their firms never make the cultural shift to becoming trusted business advisors, and their clients are left to fend for themselves. We saw too much of this during the most recent *great* recession. Happily, we were heartened by stories of small businesses that fared better because they had a Mentor Plus® trained advisor by their side.

Back in 1999, the success of the Mentor Plus® CART program caught the attention of the AICPA (American Institute of CPAs). The AICPA was launching new service lines to expand the role of accountants. One was called CPA Performance View. The AICPA identified the role of the profession in the new century as **to improve the quality of information for decision makers**. At its core, CPA Performance View was about the identification of KPIs (Key Performance Indicators) and the development of business dashboards to provide real-time decision support to business leaders. Mentor Plus® curriculum became the centerpiece of that service launch.

The training program was called Performance Measurement Plus (PMP). We trained hundreds of practitioners from partners to young shining stars. There was little doubt about the program's value, and it appeared that the profession was well positioned to expand in this direction.

However, within a couple years of launching the program, high profile accounting scandals triggered a retreat from advisory services back to ethics-focused core services. Paradigm shifters like me could only watch as the promise of business advisory services was once again placed on the back burner.

Thankfully, two leaders, under the direction of Daryl Ritchie, CEO from the Canadian firm Meyers Norris Penny (MNP), attended one of our PMP programs. MNP had the leadership, vision, and stamina to jump in with both feet to make the transition from a compliance orientation to advisory (reliance) focus. Over the course of several years, we trained in excess of 200 of MNP's shining stars on our advisory approach. MNP then licensed the curriculum, and it is now an integral part of their culture and what they call "The MNP Way." It is exciting to see how our program helped to accelerate a lot young accountants along the partner track.

MNP's commitment to living up to the moniker of trusted business advisor using the Mentor Plus® advisory framework gave us the proof and confidence we needed to re-launch our program in the United States.

Between MNP, CART firms, and other Mentor Plus® trained practitioners, it wasn't long before we were able to quantify over $100M in Level 5 services sold to small businesses across North America – despite the commonly held belief that small businesses were too fee sensitive to buy advisory services. We had evidence to the contrary; clients are not fee sensitive, they are *value sensitive*.

Upon completing the MNP engagement, it was time to update the program. We focused on the Level 5 Service framework (detailed in the book) making it leaner and more accessible to a wider audience of practitioners including CFOs, Pro Advisors, bookkeepers, management consultants, IT professionals, and budding accountants. We knew that in order for the profession to transition from **compliance to a reliance** (advisory) focus we had to make the Level 5 Service mindset, skill set, and tool set an embraceable core competency across the profession.

We re-launched our training as The Mentor Plus® M.B.A. – More Business Acumen Program. The objective is to teach practitioners how to apply their measurement skills to all areas of business performance thus enabling their clients to make intelligent, real-time, strategically aligned decisions.

Further proof we were on the right track:

At the 2013 gathering of Thought Leaders hosted by CPA Practice Magazine, 60% of the Thought Leaders felt the number one issue threatening the profession was relevance (or lack thereof). The other 40% ranked it in their top tier of issues.

There doesn't seem to be any question that accountants have to change the way they deliver value to the clients they serve. And yet, even with profession-wide efforts to re-brand the profession as trusted business advisors, progress has been very slow.

So why haven't we made more progress in this area over the past 20 years? I believe it's because the profession has failed to define what it *really* means to be a trusted business advisor. In spite of how many practitioners claim they are trusted business advisors, there are a lot of accountants who fall short of the definition; they would be better described as *trusted accounting technicians*.

The other obstacle, in my opinion, is the profession has yet to adopt a standardized framework for doing advisory work. Clients understand what tax returns, financial statements, and audits are all about. But "advisory services"? They have no real idea what it means.

How can we expect clients to embrace a new brand we have yet to define?

Buckminster Fuller said it best,

"If you want to teach people a new way of thinking, don't bother trying to teach them. Instead, give them a tool, the use of which will lead to new ways of thinking."

The "tool" is the Level 5 Service framework. I've written white papers and articles on this subject for years, so why write this book? I believe the profession is finally reaching a tipping point. Today, market conditions and competition are putting enormous pressure on the profession to move in a new direction.

This year, the AICPA collaborated with Dr. Geoffrey Moore, noted author of *Crossing the Chasm* and *Escape Velocity: Free Your Company's Future from the Pull of the Past,* to evaluate the current state and future of the profession. A powerful white paper resulted from that collaboration: *Transforming Client Services*. (Go to www.cpa.com to download.)

Dr. Moore contends there are three mega trends driving the profession:

1) **Digitalization – transitioning information to the digital environment.**
2) **Virtualization – transitioning services to the cloud. and**
3) **Transformation – transitioning client relationships from compliance to reliance *(my words)*.**

Many firms are already on board with scanning, work-flow, portals, mobile technology, and cloud computing, but for every 1,000 firms on track with Digitalization and Virtualization, only a handful of firms are focused on Transformation.

However good a technician you may be and however adept your firm is at adopting new technology, if you aren't helping clients improve their business

performance, your best days may be behind you. Your real competitors are those closing the gap between trusted accounting technician and trusted business advisor.

My hope is after reading this book you'll be inspired to expand your mindset, skill set, and tool set to help your clients improve their business performance. Whether you're inspired to change by your own vision or change is forced upon you, as is the case in this story, my hope is that you'll embrace it for the opportunity it affords.

Although this story chronicles a great deal of change over the course of one year, it's merely a snapshot. The foundation and motivation for change was already in place, and the continual reinforcement of the Level 5 Service model continues long after the story ends. Nonetheless, you might begin to question if it is possible to make a significant shift in your firm's culture in such a short time frame. As Henry Ford said, *"If you think you can do a thing or think you can't do a thing, you're right."*

I dream of a day when Level 5 Advisors are actively teaching business owners how to work smarter, not harder; how to thrive, not just survive. Level 5 Advisors could significantly improve the quality of life for millions of small business owners and their employees. I also envision a day when accounting students around the world are taught the Level 5 Service framework so they enter the profession already hardwired with trusted business advisor skills and all the efforts to re-brand the profession will finally take hold.

Our goal

We're all about strengthening our economy *one accountant at a time* via Level 5 Service. Those Level 5 Advisors will then be in a position to help strengthen our economy *one business at a time*. Let's do the math: if one accountant/advisor has a relationship with an average of 50 business clients, and we train just 10,000 accountants/advisors, the result is half a million businesses with a greater chance of success. If each of those businesses then hires two new employees, that's a million new jobs created because we all committed to teaching small business owners the fundamentals of a well-run business. Our BHAG (Big Hairy Audacious Goal from James Collins' book ***Good to Great***) is to build an army of Level 5 Advisors to significantly impact the health of our economy.

Together we CAN make a difference!

Edi Osborne, CEO, Mentor Plus

If everyone is moving forward together, then success takes care of itself.

Henry Ford

Firm

Forward

*The most dangerous leadership myth is that leaders
are born – that there is a genetic factor to leadership.
This myth asserts that people simply either have
certain charismatic qualities or not.
That's nonsense; in fact, the opposite is true.
Leaders are made rather than born.*

Warren G. Bennis

Introduction

My name is Bennett Stewart. I always thought my last name should be my first and my first my last, but my mom's maiden name was Bennett, and she insisted that it worked just fine as either. At least that's what she reminded me every first day of school when the teachers would invariably call me Stewart Bennett, and the kids would laugh and call me "Stewie." To avoid the inevitable teasing that came with that, the summer between 7th and 8th grade (shortly after my dad died) *Bennett* went the way of my old gym clothes, and I became Bennie. There were already two Bens in my school. I'm not sure if Bennie is any better than Stewie; for me it was about taking charge of my own destiny.

I'm an involved father, attentive husband, grateful son, avid football fan, second-rate golfer, and first-class accountant. I passed the CPA exam on the first try, made it through 21 tax seasons, and met more 15th of the month deadlines than I can count. I've never considered myself to be a traditional accountant and have always colored outside the lines just enough to avoid the stereotype. Still, looking at the totality of my professional career, however much I wanted to break the mold I ended up bending to the status quo even when I knew it was not in my best interest or that of my clients.

I am going to tell you a story, a story about my life and the accounting firm where I work. We all have "moments of truth" at different times in our lives. Often there is a catalyst event that forever changes the trajectory of our lives. This was mine.

You should always know when
you're shifting gears in life.
You should leave your era;
it should never leave you.

Leontyne Price

Our Moment of Truth

It started like any Friday morning partner meeting. The five of us sat down to review the billings, hours, and work in progress, but before we could even go down that road, Tom, our managing partner, announced there was serious business to discuss.

Tom is 61. He's been a great mentor to me over the years. It was common knowledge I was being groomed to be the next managing partner, but there was no formal succession plan in place. This past tax season, Tom had looked worn down every day except for one: April 15th, when he headed out the door for two weeks of fly fishing in Montana. When he returned on May 1st, he looked a little more rested, but by the 15th of May he was starting to wear down again.

Today Tom looked more stressed than ever. There had been rumblings around the office during the week, but I had been so busy on an audit that the gravity of our situation didn't hit me until Tom spoke.

"As you know, Hallstrom, Inc., was bought by a multi-national conglomerate. We're already winding down and transitioning files to the parent company." Tom continued, "In addition, Star Industries informed us yesterday morning that they are planning on moving their business to another firm."

You could've heard a pin drop. Those two accounts added up to nearly 20% of our business; it was a big hit by any firm's standards.

"And if that wasn't enough, Katie Thomas and Mark Perish gave notice late yesterday. They plan to start their own practice. I don't need to tell you how difficult it's going to be to replace them. I don't know if we can. They were two of our best managers."

The room was quiet as we processed the information. The pencil pushers, Howard and Newton (a.k.a Newt) saw a bright side to Katie and Mark's exodus: The reduction in payroll would help offset lost revenues. They may have found a silver lining, but Tom's face told the real story. Losing a big client is always hard, but you can somehow console yourself that it was inevitable given the buyout. But losing Star Industries along with Katie and Mark felt like a three-strikes-you're-out kind of blow.

A few years back, we spent a fortune, at least by our standards, for an outside facilitator to lead our partner retreat. We had a knack for coming away from retreats with grand ideas but we were short on follow-through. We thought having a facilitator would somehow give us the secret formula or wave a magic wand that would make the difference. At the end of the session, we had the same to-do list as the year before: a formal partner development track, a structured succession plan, and expanded advisory services.

In our defense, it had been a tough couple of years. We had weathered the economic downturn with a few bumps and bruises, but, all in all, we were doing okay. I'll admit we didn't get the retreat initiatives up and running as hoped, but we got our accounting work done, met deadlines, and managed to bring in a few new clients along the way. Like I said, we thought we were doing okay, until Tom opened his mouth. Then our false sense of security for having maintained the status quo blew up in our faces.

Tom went on to say feedback from the lost client and the two managers revealed a troubling trend. "It turns out they're leaving for different, but related reasons. You all know the CEO of Star Industries, Jack Marshall. He said they're leaving because he wants an accounting firm that is more proactive and focused on helping him grow his business. He pointed to the recession and how disappointed he was that we hadn't done more to help him respond to the downturn.

"Katie and Mark also talked about the lack of proactive guidance and professional development in the firm. Mark was especially vocal about the lack of accountability amongst the partner group to follow through on commitments." Tom finished by telling us that Katie was frustrated by the lack of proactive effort to help our clients as they were struggling through the recession. Not being proactive seemed to be the common thread.

No one likes bad news, but this news was especially painful because it was an indictment on our lack of follow through on the initiatives we'd committed to. The initiatives had been pushed aside year after year because we were always so busy. The thought that we'd been lulled into thinking being busy was somehow a higher priority than moving the firm forward really stung. We'd built our entire firm culture around a faulty definition of success, and I knew I was partly to blame for it.

Then I remembered having lunch with Katie nearly a year ago. She talked about how several of our clients were having cash flow issues, and she asked for my permission to analyze their cash flow and stress test their financial assumptions. Star Industries had been among those on her target list. I could tell she was hesitant to ask, and it should have hit me then that she'd seen the problem, knew how to solve it, and I was in the way. But I'd just come from a partner meeting where we reviewed our accounts receivable and we were all on high alert to improve our own cash flow. I told Katie to focus on clients who could pay our bill not those falling behind. If only I could take those words back.

Likewise when I'd sat down with Mark at the end of our

last audit, he wanted to talk about becoming a partner. He asked me, point blank, what the game plan was for Katie and him, given their seniority as managers. Mark and Katie had been to an emerging leaders conference – a conference we sent them to – that talked about firms needing to have a formal path to partnership so young people wouldn't become discouraged and strike out on their own. Everything he said made sense. I had wished for a formal partner track like he described when I joined the firm. Even now, I wondered when Tom would *ever* step down. Thinking back, Mark gave the firm the chance to step up, and we failed him. It was so obvious, anyone should have seen it. If I were a Twitter geek, I would have tweeted: #firmfail.

Sharon, our newest partner as of four years ago, had offered up similar conversations she'd had with both Katie and Mark. But Sharon had become somewhat of a team champion, something that routinely put her at loggerheads with Howard and Newt, so I hadn't taken it as seriously as I should have. How could we have been so blind? No mystery. We were busy, flat out, barely keeping up with the workload, focused on adopting new technologies, and we made flawed assumptions about young talent having "faith" in the firm. These shortsighted assumptions were rooted in our *good-old-days* mindset when younger staff didn't push so hard and were grateful to just be acknowledged once in a while. That's the kind of firm culture I started out in, but things had changed. For the past several years, experts at every conference warned us of the need for a new way to manage the Next Gen accountant. Thinking we were immune, we'd turned a blind eye to all the signs and symptoms of discontent right under our noses.

Over the years, Sharon and I had spoken about the expectations of younger staff. The "Y" generation needed a lot more one-on-one coaching and mentoring than we ever got. For Sharon, that extra handholding was a point of frustration; she even resisted becoming a partner because of it. She was happy to work hard so long as she could walk out the door to play even harder. The idea that she would be a role model and *coach* others in the firm made her laugh and a bit uncomfortable.

In spite of her reluctance, she grew into the role of partner and garnered the respect of the team for her no-nonsense approach. For someone who didn't want others looking up to her, she'd achieved "cult-hero" status as a champion for the team.

One incident in particular had elevated her to legendary status among the staff. Howard had gone out to visit a client, to deliver financial statements. The client pointed out a significant error in the balance sheet, and Howard returned to the office enraged, determined to berate the manager who'd prepared the documents. It was determined later on that the error had come from Howard, but he wouldn't hear it. He kept at it. Sharon let it go on for a couple minutes before stepping in. To be fair, she tried to handle it quietly at first by inviting Howard to step into her office. Howard, intent on berating the manager for embarrassing him in front of a client, ignored her.

I wasn't there, but I've heard the story so many times, I can see it in my mind's eye. According to team legend, Sharon grew a foot taller in a matter of seconds, got right up in Howard's face, and laid into him for five minutes straight. She cited numerous examples and let Howard know, in no uncertain terms, she wasn't going to tolerate his bullying any longer. Howard was stunned – Margaret told me his mouth kept opening and closing like a fish. Finally, he gave up, walked back to his office, and shut the door. Sharon went back to her office and not another word was said. Sharon and Howard have been in a cordial Mexican standoff ever since.

After some awkward silence, Howard started fuming about non-competes and lawsuits. Sharon bristled a bit, then smiled when Tom quickly cut him off.

"Those are valid concerns we'll need to address but, frankly, not today; that's the least of our worries." Thankfully Tom recommended we cut the meeting short with the commitment to come back together on Monday prepared to address three questions:

1) How are we going to replace the lost revenues?
2) How are we going to keep clients from leaving?
3) How are we going to replace Mark and Katie?

I didn't realize it that day, but those three questions would eventually lead me to one answer: Level 5 Service.

Family Wisdom

An accident on the highway resulted in an especially long, quiet ride home, probably a good thing given my mood. Pulling into the driveway, I tried to summon up the energy to handle the chaos that was our life. I would have loved an hour or two with a glass or three of my favorite wine, but there was no time for that. This was Friday night, and our son, Chris, was on the varsity football team. Our night was tightly scheduled: getting to the game, a shift at the concession stand, keeping our two little girls out of trouble, and, if I was lucky, I might actually get to watch Chris play. We ended up winning, and that meant celebratory pizza and ice cream.

Once Caroline and Susie (ages 6 and 4) were tucked into bed, I poured myself the long awaited glass of wine and settled into my favorite spot on the couch. I thought about turning on the TV to catch up on some programs we'd recorded earlier in the week. There's one show in particular I enjoy watching: a show where entrepreneurs pitch their products and ideas to investors in the hopes of raising capital. I've always been intrigued by the innovations people come up with. Conversely, I'm often shocked at how often they get turned down because they lack the basic financial acumen to answer the investors' questions. It makes me wonder about their accountant (or lack thereof). But I just couldn't bring myself to disturb the silence. Anna poured herself a glass and refilled mine before she sat down beside me.

Anna's smart – and I mean *very* smart. She's one of those people you know are smart even when they haven't spoken yet, and she's purposeful in everything she does. We met in college. I noticed her maneuvering through the busy quad, bobbing and weaving like a prizefighter, smiling all the while like she was having the best day of

31

her life. She was beautiful then and she still is, but I was also attracted to her energy. She never had that "lost" or "I'm late" air about her, like the other students.

Each day I would try to position myself in her path to see if I could catch her attention. It took a couple weeks because I was a little shy back then. Finally, a rainy day turned out to be my saving grace. The weatherman had said there was only a 30% chance of showers so Anna wasn't carrying an umbrella. Knowing her as I do now, it wasn't a mistake but a calculated risk. Thank you, Mr. Weatherman! I saw my opening and I took it, literally, *borrowing* an umbrella from outside one of the classrooms and running over to her. I sidled up to her left side, put the umbrella between us, and the rest is history.I studied accounting; Anna studied biochemistry. We had our lives planned out. I'd become an accountant; she'd become a research scientist. We'd graduate, get married, and, while I worked, Anna would get her PhD. We'd have three children, find a home in a great neighborhood with great schools, and live happily ever after. So far, so good.

Despite a great personal life, I was pretty bummed about what was happening at the firm. The announcements at the partners' meeting should have come as a shock, but I wasn't surprised. I'd been struggling with my own issues about the firm's direction. Losing Star Industries was hard, but losing Mark and Katie was personal. I felt like I had failed them and, in the process, failed myself.

In her quiet way, Anna teased the day's events out of me. She had a gift for asking the right questions to get to the heart of a problem; it makes her a talented researcher and a great mom. She never assumes; she just keeps asking questions until a solution reveals itself, while remaining open to the idea there may be more than one right answer.

She followed the same questioning discipline teaching our

kids to make better decisions, and is so good at it that our son has a special nickname for her. A couple of years ago, he came home after his humanities class and dubbed his mom Socrates, affectionately known as Soc-Mom to his friends. Anna laughed and doing what she does best, asked Chris some questions.

"Who is Socrates, and why do you think I deserve that name?"

With a small giggle and roll of the eyes, he said, "He's just like you, Mom. He doesn't tell people what to do. He uses questions to teach people how to think about things so they can figure it out for themselves."

Anna wasn't finished, "Why would Socrates want people to learn how to think? Wouldn't it be easier just to tell people what to do?"

"If you don't know how to ask questions and think about things, you won't learn to trust your own judgment," replied Chris. As Anna was about to ask another question, Chris stopped her, "Enough, Socrates. No more questions, please."

From the time Chris was in pre-school, Anna never asked "What did you learn in school today?" Instead, she took a different tack, "What questions did you ask today?" Anna has a theory about what advances societies: she believes that a curious mind is critical to our survival as a species. If we accept status quo as our only reality there is no room for other possibilities. She's done her best to cultivate our children's curiosity.

Her unrestrained curiosity was such a stark contrast from the accounting profession: we tend to put more value on being an expert (and being right) than being curious. We often shy away from innovation and exploration of new ideas and avoid asking questions we don't already have the answer to. What's the saying? "It takes five *why* questions to get to the heart of a problem."

Most of us stop asking *why* questions at about age three because it's trained out of us. Weary parents, myself included, take the "because I said so, that's why" easy way out.

Thankfully, Anna a.k.a. Soc-Mom, took pity on me and let me just exhale all that had been bottled up inside since the partner meeting. I shared Tom's questions from the meeting. By the time Anna had led me through some focused questions of her own, I knew I had to reframe Tom's questions from being reactive to more strategically focused. She was quiet for a moment, then she asked one final question before we finished our wine and headed off to bed. I added it to my list.

My Focus:
How to build revenues?
How to keep clients happy?
How to keep the team happy?
If we were starting the firm from scratch, what would we do differently?

Lessons Learned

The wine and the busy day caught up with me, so Anna's question didn't get much attention before I crashed. However, the question did sink into my subconscious and into my dreams.

I was 22-years-old and finishing up my last semester in college when I went to a job fair. My accounting professor recommended I check out what different firms had to offer. Armed with great recommendations from my professor and the firm internship that year, I got several offers, including one from the firm I interned at, Harrison & Co.

As exciting and prestigious as working for a multinational firm sounded, I decided a smaller firm was a better fit for me, working with small businesses in my own hometown. Plus, we needed stability so Anna could stay on track with her PhD. Anna would have adjusted her plans, but I didn't want her to have to. And I'd always loved the small businesses in our town. The firm I interned with was a known quantity, and I genuinely liked the people, especially Tom Harrison.

My love of small business comes from my dad. He was an entrepreneur who owned an insurance agency that served (I swear) every single person within 100 miles. At least that's what it felt like. I remember going out on calls with him (often on weekends and evenings) to visit clients at their farms, factories, stores, offices, and even in their homes. When we walked down the street, he knew everyone's name, and they knew his.

"Hey there, Mike, how are ya?" he'd say. "How are Betty and the kids? How's Sean doing at college?" I was always amazed at how my dad knew the names of all of his clients' children and even their pets. He remembered birthdays and anniversaries and even sent out sympathy cards when Fido or kitty passed away.

I asked him once why he didn't just let the clients come to his office. He said, "If you really want to serve someone's needs, you have to step into their world to *see* the need." I didn't appreciate it then, but looking back, my dad was a brilliant businessman: he would always take note of a new piece of equipment or expanded space or a frail parent during his visits, observations that often led to more business opportunities.

I knew of a certain store owner, who will remain nameless, that was not a client, and I asked my dad why we didn't go visit that store and make him one. My dad grew quiet for a moment, then looked me straight in the eye and said, "Son, in your life you'll meet people who are always looking to gain some advantage over others, whether it be undeserved discounts or other concessions. You can spend a lifetime trying to please those people and never succeed. Meanwhile, you're leaving the people who are honest and fair starving for help. I decided long ago to spend *my* time feeding the starving crowd." To explain what he meant by "starving crowd" he shared this story.

Three successful entrepreneurs were asked the question, "If you were starting a restaurant and could claim any competitive advantage, what would you choose?"

The first replied, "Location, location, location. You have to have a good location with a lot of foot traffic."

The second replied, "People, people, people. Without the right chefs and wait-staff your venture will fail."

The third pondered for a moment. He acknowledged how important both location and people are but said, "I would give all that up for one thing... A starving crowd."

My dad went on to say that small businesses are the backbone of our economy and the heartbeat of our community, and they're starving for attention. Whenever Dad went out prospecting for new business, he looked for those hungry for peace of mind. My dad always said he was in the peace of mind business, not insurance sales. As it turns out, I'm in the peace of mind business, too.

I loved my dad, he taught me so much. He had a heart attack when I was 12. One minute he was mowing the lawn, the next he was gone. I still miss him every day. As you would expect, my dad had a good life insurance policy, so my mom and I were able to live comfortably. But even with the nest egg my dad set up for her, my mom continued teaching elementary school until our son was born. There was just something about having a grandchild that made her want to quit work and become a full time grandma, and it was a godsend for us. Mom wanted nothing more than to babysit the kids while Anna and I worked. We count our blessings every day for Mom's love and support.

I had a charmed life with nothing to complain about, and yet something wasn't working for me. That Friday morning partner meeting was a personal and professional wake-up call. Time to ask the questions I had been too busy (or scared) to ask. Now I had no choice.

For the past several months, I'd had a recurring dream about doors. Nearly every dream included a door: one door closing, some opening, others waiting for me to make a choice. Like Monty Hall's "Let's Make a Deal," I often woke up wondering what was behind the doors I *didn't* choose. I was in a deep sleep when I heard the voices of my sweet girls, "Daddy, Daddy, DAAAADDDDY wake-up! It's time to get ready for the party. We need you to put up the twinkle lights."

Party? It had completely slipped my mind. This was my sister-in-law Karen's birthday, and we were hosting a surprise party that evening.

Anna had let me sleep in as long as she could before dispatching the girls to *gently* wake me up. I showered like a sailor and ran downstairs to find my mom (a.k.a. Nomi) in the kitchen helping Anna with food prep. Nomi was Chris' toddler blending of Naomi and Nana. A quick kiss on the cheek, a piece of toast shoved into my mouth, and I was out the back door where I found my father-in-law, Carl, ladder in hand and lights strung round him like a Christmas tree. He'd done his best to keep the girls occupied before calling for backup. I couldn't believe I'd slept so late, but I was still exhausted, and it was as much emotional as physical.

Without ever forcing the issue, Carl had become both a father figure and best friend. Like his daughter, he always had a warm smile and open heart. He was a retired scientist, enjoying his retirement years playing golf and helping his two daughters keep their husbands in line. I'm kidding, mostly, but he was always there setting the right example. Anna's mom had passed away from cancer two years before. Carl was by her side every waking moment until the very end. Even though he was tired to the bone, it never affected his attitude. Each day was a new (and possibly his last) day with his beloved Lydia.

When Lydia passed away, I half expected Carl to fall apart, but he didn't. We all watched carefully for signs of depression, but there were none. He missed her terribly, but somehow he found reasons to be happy in spite of his grief.

I'm not much of a golfer, but for Father's Day last year Anna signed Carl and me up for a week long golf clinic in Texas. Texas in June, what were we thinking? We weren't. We'd start out at dawn to be done by noon. That left room for some lazy afternoons by the pool and a pitcher of ice cold beer-margaritas (genius combination, just sayin').

I'm not sure my golf swing improved much but I gained an even greater appreciation for Carl. A scratch golfer, Carl could have taught the clinic, but he was always humble and excited about learning any new technique. Anna's purposefulness and disposition comes from her dad. Carl would occasionally hit a bad shot and bogey a hole, but he never got discouraged. Not even a double bogey could throw him off. He never focused on the last hole, only the one ahead, each hole like a new game.

On one of our lazy afternoons by the pool, Carl shared a story about when his lab burned down, back in the days before computers and backup drives. His lab equipment, notes, and all of his documented experiments were gone. I expected him to lament a truly devastating blow to his research, but, in typical Carl fashion, he talked of his excitement: he got to start over without the constraints of the past. He explained how easy it was to continue down a path even when we know it may not be the right one – letting go of old beliefs to make room for new possibilities was that hard. He said, "Nothing clears the way for a fresh start like a good bonfire."

I was thinking of that conversation by the pool as we were stringing the patio lights. With the girls inside helping Anna and Nomi with the party preparations, Carl and I had a few quiet moments to talk, and I shared the events of the day before. I put up a brave front, calling it a catalyst for good, but Carl knew me too well and could read the truth on my face.

Carl asked a few simple questions that helped me refocus:

"Is it possible to find another client to replace Star Industries? Is it possible to find or develop some managers to replace the two who left?"

"Of course we can replace them," I said.

"So all is not lost, right?"

I nodded, but the look on my face betrayed me.

Carl said, "In my experience, when the reaction is greater than the consequences of a circumstance warrant, there is usually something hidden beneath the surface that needs to be revealed."

"Like what?" I asked.

"You're taking Mark and Katie's exit so personally. Is it possible you're just a wee bit jealous?"

"Jealous, are you nuts? They're starting from scratch, building infrastructure, marketing, hiring, training, managing the firm, everything. They have no idea what lies ahead of them."

Carl persisted. "They might not anticipate everything they'll have to cope with, but they probably have a good idea of the challenges ahead, don't you think? And still, they walked away from a great firm, right?"

"A great firm? Maybe. We're good accountants, but I'm not sure we're a great firm. A great firm would have put a better succession strategy together. A great firm would have gone out and helped struggling clients. Heck, a great firm would have done more to keep their clients from struggling in the first place. A great firm–"

"Sorry to interrupt, you're on quite a roll, but it sure sounds like Mark and Katie made a pretty reasonable choice given the circumstances. It's almost like you left them no choice."

"Ouch, Carl. When you put it like that, it hurts. They had a choice. They could have been more vocal and given us some time to respond."

"Really? Didn't you tell me about conversations when Mark and Katie stated their cases, and voiced their concerns to you and your partners?"

"Yeah, they did talk to us. I guess we weren't listening. I feel like I failed them. But honestly, how could I tell them things were going to improve when I was just as frustrated as they were?"

"How long have they been with the firm?"

"Mark joined us right out of school so that's nine years. Katie worked for another firm for four years and has been with us the last six."

"Are they qualified to be partners?"

"As much or more than I was. The real rub is that they weren't asking to be made partners immediately. They just wanted to know what the plan and timeline looked like. The truth is they were asking the same kinds of questions I was asking myself about becoming managing partner."

Just then, Anna stuck her head out the backdoor, "Don't forget to set up the tables and chairs – the girls will be out in a few minutes to start decorating." Carl glanced at his watch and smiled at what was about to happen. I'd left my cell phone upstairs and lost track of time. Carl's smile reminded me that we were in for a little treat.

We had a family ritual where we all did chores together

41

on Saturday mornings, including car washing, yard work, laundry, toy clean up, room straightening, and the like. Anna would put on some of her favorite Motown hits from the 60s, and we would dance around and sing, getting the chores done. Anna had a gift for making even the most laborious jobs fun. This routine started during tax season when Chris was a toddler. Anna wanted to find a way to distract Chris from the fact that his daddy would disappear every Saturday from February through April 15th. I hated Saturdays in the office during tax season, knowing what I was missing out on.

In recent years, after a week of football practice and Friday night games, tired, sore, and bruised, we excused Chris from Saturday morning chores during football season. This was his recovery time, and we let him sleep until noon. His little sisters took great joy in waking him up, running and jumping on him when Anna gave them the go ahead. Chris always pretended to be annoyed, but, knowing it was coming, he would often set his alarm to wake up a few minutes before the girls were due and would launch an ambush.

Today was no different. Anna had reminded him about the party prep with a little note on his pillow, to be found when he got home from the game. Anna was famous for her well-placed, thoughtful notes. By the time Caroline and Susie came to his room, Chris had already showered and was dressed, waiting under the covers for the assault. He jumped up before the girls even got to the bed. You could almost set your watch by it: the joyful giggles and squeals of delight from the girls were worth listening for. Carl and Nomi were well acquainted with the ritual. Noon on Saturdays was always guaranteed to bring a smile, whatever your state of mind happened to be.

Funny how a little thing like our Saturday morning wake-up routine could ground me so quickly. I was a lucky guy. Now, if I could just find as much fulfillment in my work.

Perspective

With the patio ready for the party, there was a lull in the action while the girls laid down for their afternoon "quiet time." I went upstairs and found several messages on my cell: one from Tom, two from Sharon, and an e-mail from Mark and Katie. I sat down in my little home/office, just off our bedroom and braced myself. Tom's text was quite short, "Can we meet tomorrow? I really need to talk to you." Sharon's was similar except she wanted to talk over the phone sometime over the weekend, which didn't surprise me because she was usually on a road trip.

Mark and Katie's e-mail was not so brief.

Dear Bennie,

We are writing this to you and you alone. We want you to know how much we have appreciated working with you over the years. You've been a great mentor and a true friend. You always went out of your way to include us in client engagements even when the other partners couldn't understand why you kept taking us out into the field with you. We know it was difficult to justify the billings, but your investment in our professional development was a big reason why we stayed as long as we did.

Those times in the field, watching you work your magic with clients, raised our expectations that the firm, as a whole, would move in the direction of doing more advisory work. A single "field trip" taught us more about real business issues than six months of sitting in the office cranking out financial statements or tax returns.

Our decision to leave the firm is in no way a reflection on you, but rather of the lack of direction and focus of the firm in general. We have no intention of targeting any current work the firm is providing so you can let the partners know they can chill out on that front.

To be totally candid, there's no reason to target accounting work away from the firm; the firm does excellent work, and we want the clients to continue to benefit from having their compliance work done by the firm. The focus of our firm will be advisory work. Both our spouses are behind us 100%. This gives us a few months to get up and running on a virtual basis before taking on significant overhead. Although it may not seem possible right now, our hope is that the firm will not see us as the enemy but as an ally. We believe our complimentary advisory focus would allow for a very positive synergistic relationship between our two firms.

In the spirit of cooperation, if there is anything we can do to support the transfer of work to others in the firm, don't hesitate to contact us. We told all of this to Tom on Thursday evening when we met with him. But he seemed to be operating on autopilot when he escorted us to our offices to clean out our personal belongings and exit the building. We'd seen it before so we knew it was coming. In fact, we spent the last month making sure all the client files were up to date and any work in progress was closed out (as best we could). It was just hard to leave without really explaining our intentions to everyone and parting on amicable terms. Hopefully we can rewind the clock a bit with this e-mail.

Again, thank you for all that you've done for us over the years. We really appreciate you and all the fighting you did on our behalf along the way. Please pass on our best wishes to Anna and the kids. We hope we'll see you around town and it's not too awkward.

All our best,

Mark and Katie

P.S. We're just putting this out there. If you had taken over leadership of the firm five years ago (or were taking the helm now), we wouldn't be having this discussion. If things don't end up going in the direction you're hoping for, we would welcome you with open arms into our new venture.

I was numb. I was sad. I was mad as I read the e-mail. Not mad at Mark and Katie, but mad at myself for not being more assertive about what I believe, what I know, was the right direction for our firm.

And as Carl had wisely observed, I was also jealous.

Mark and Katie were doing exactly what I wanted to be doing, and they knew it. Several of us in the firm had attended training a couple years ago to learn how to deliver Level 5 Service, but we hadn't completely bought into the full potential.

Full potential?

Hell, we grasped the mindset, but dropped the ball on implementation. Ironically, it was that mindset that had set this inevitably in motion.

Mark and Katie clearly got it, and they were running with it.

I texted Tom that we could meet on Sunday but I needed to check with Anna about the timing. As I sat in my office, the binder from the Level 5 Service training we attended begged for some long overdue attention.

Unless you're willing to have a go, fail miserably, and have another go, success won't happen.

Phillip Adams

More Than One Surprise

We were ready for the party, and the guest room was set up for Karen and Josh to stay over. The kids would be camped out in the basement rumpus room, aptly named years earlier by Peter, Josh, and Karen's oldest. Peter was about seven years old when he named the rumpus room "Bennie-Annas" just like the restaurant Benihana. He thought it was so funny that a restaurant had been named after his aunt and uncle. From then on, our kids picked up on it and always welcomed their friends to BennieAnna's, although the reference to the restaurant was lost on Caroline and Susie.

As planned, all the guests arrived early. We waited, and as Josh, Karen, and their three boys walked through the door, we all yelled, "SURPRISE!" Karen was blown away. She never expected a surprise party, because she'd made it clear she didn't want a fuss for her 40th. She could protest as much as she wanted, but once Anna and Carl set their mind to something, there was no stopping them.

After the kids headed downstairs for the campout, the party went from a roar to a hum, giving me a few minutes to catch up with Josh. I always enjoyed the tale of his latest conquest. In addition to being a great brother-in-law and friend, he is also a client. I've done his taxes for 15 years, watching his company grow from a one man shop to over 250 employees. Over the years, we've talked shop, but mostly I've listened to Josh as he talked about his challenges and victories.

With a little liquid courage in me, I asked Josh a very pointed question. "Would you consider our firm to be your most trusted business advisor?"

Josh smiled and said, "Why are you asking?"

I continued, "One of our larger clients is leaving the firm because we weren't proactive enough helping him navigate the recession."

"I see. Do you want the truth, or do you want to feel good?"

"I want the truth."

"I consider you guys to be good – even great – accounting technicians, but not my most trusted business advisor."

"Technicians?"

"Yes, technicians. I have a tremendous amount of confidence in your accounting services, but when it comes to real business advice beyond my financial or accounting needs, I couldn't say one way or the other. It's not that you've ever done anything wrong, just that the firm has never done anything outside of accounting and tax work."

I took a deep breath. I felt myself getting defensive and had to consciously stop my frustration from contaminating the conversation.

"Is there someone else you consider your most trusted business advisor?"

"No, not one person. I'd say two, maybe three consultants over the years really made a difference in the transformation and direction of my business. I introduced you to one of them a few months back, when we ran into each other at The Grill on 4th St. Do you remember Paul Henry?"

"Yes, I remember Paul. What makes him your trusted business advisor?"

"Paul has a knack for asking me questions to make me

really examine my leadership choices and the performance of our company." He paused, then said, "Bennie, you know I love you like a brother, right? We've always been straight with each other. I'm going to tell you what business owners really think about their CPA. Can you handle that?"

"Sure, I can handle it." I couldn't imagine he could say anything that would really rock me to the core. I'd heard it all before: bean counters, nerds, and the like.

"You asked, so here goes. CPAs are great. They're great at accounting, auditing, and tax preparation. They're also good at pointing out what's wrong with our numbers – after the fact. Members in my CEO Forum refer to their CPAs as Monday morning quarterbacks. With very few exceptions, accountants are so caught up on accuracy, they forget to ask if the information they provide is relevant.

Honestly, every set of financial statements I get from your office is a regurgitation of what I can pull from my own system. In fact, our general ledger and internal management reports guide my decisions far more than the formal financial statements you guys provide. One of the first things Paul had me do was restructure our chart of accounts to produce departmental profit/loss statements that feed into a dashboard for all my managers. That one suggestion alone has made a world of difference in how my leadership team manages and evaluates the performance of the company."

He stopped again to see how I was taking it, then continued, "Do you know what one of your managers said when our controller explained our new chart of accounts? He said it was going to cost us more for tax prep because he would have to reorganize the information back to the old format to get my taxes prepared."

I cringed. "Sorry 'bout that. I can tell that comment didn't go over well. I really appreciate your honesty."

"Every entrepreneur I know complains about their CPA firm at some time or another, so don't feel too badly. We accept the status quo and lower our expectations accordingly. Don't get me wrong, we love 'em and trust 'em, but we don't expect much in the way of management advice. Paul Henry and I even talked about this. He said management consultants are capitalizing on accountants' general resistance to change. Now, if I were running an accounting firm, I'd be focused on that low level of expectations and make it a priority to rise above. A good firm like Harrison & Co. could easily differentiate itself in the marketplace, assuming you put the needs of entrepreneurs front and center, instead of focusing so much on recording history. Still, as good as Paul Henry is, he doesn't have your financial chops, Bennie."

"Thanks for saying that. I was starting to wonder if you stayed with us all these years just because we're related."

"To be honest, that's probably a good part of it. But, in my mind, you aren't a typical CPA. When I've asked you to help me with special projects, you've always *exceeded* my expectations. I just wish that rather than waiting for me to ask for help, you were more proactive."

There was that word again.

"My dad always said, 'Never sell clients more than they need or less than they want.' We're good at filling the tax and accounting needs of our clients, but it seems we're missing the boat on what they really want. Dad would say, 'It comes down to relationships. If you care enough to create a relationship with a client then you should care enough to help them in any and every way you can.'

"Dad never hesitated about jumping in and helping a

client think through a problem or helping them find the resources to get the job done. He started the town's first business networking group – not that he needed the business – although it brought him more. He genuinely liked matching his clients' needs with the services of others, and they saw real value in that."

Josh thought for a moment, then said, "From everything I've heard about your dad over the years, Bennie, it sounds like you just need to follow his example."

With so many thoughts rumbling through my head, I slept fitfully that night. And with Karen and Josh in town, along with their three boys, there was a lot of commotion on Sunday morning. The girls had a day of fun activities planned, and the boys, Chris included, headed out the door to play miniature golf. I let Chris in on the situation at work and begged off from golf in favor of meeting with Tom and following up with Sharon.

With a concerned look, Chris asked, "Are you going to be alright, Dad?" I gave him a big hug and reassured him that this was just a normal business hiccup and I'd be fine. I may have convinced Chris, but I certainly wasn't. To tell the truth, this hiccup felt more like a convulsion.

You don't grow companies.
You grow people and people grow companies.

Author unknown

A Fresh Start

We met at the office at noon. Tom was already set up in the conference room with coffee waiting for me. He looked tired. Lately, he always looked tired. Without delay, Tom started right in.

"Bennie, it's time."

"Time for what?" I asked.

"It's time for you to take over as managing partner. It's time for some new energy and a paradigm shift. All those Friday afternoon beers and conversations about what you envision for the future of the profession were a very polite way of trying to influence the direction of the firm."

"Whoa, wait a minute. Hang on, Tom. You know I've always respected you and your leadership. You've been a great mentor for me. Everything I know about being a good accountant, I learned from you."

"The operative word being 'accountant.' Yes, I know I'm a good accountant. Hell, I'm a *great* accountant. But that's not what the future of the profession is calling for or what this firm needs. The profession is changing – we see it every day – and only those who can make accounting services more relevant to the needs of business owners will thrive in the future. No more lip service about being a trusted business advisor. It's time we lived up to that title. Don't you agree?"

I sat there, my heart beating a million miles an hour. The old phrase "Be careful what you wish for" echoing in my head. This was the moment I'd been waiting on for years. But now that it had arrived, I was overwhelmed at the prospect of stepping into Tom's shoes, just as we seemed to be unraveling.

"What about Howard and Newt? Are they on board with this?"

"I've already spoken with them; Sharon, too. We're all in agreement. Effective immediately, *you* are the new managing partner."

"Just like that, so fast? What about –"

Before I could even finish the question, Tom interrupted, "Look, Bennie, we both know what's at stake now. I should have done a better job with this transition, but it is what it is. I'm not going anywhere. I'll be here to help with anything you need, but we need to make a statement to the team, our clients, and, yes, Jack Marshall at Star Industries, that we aren't stuck in the past and are moving the firm forward. It's your future, Bennie, not mine. I want to continue to work in the firm, but I am going to accept my retirement option in a few months and gracefully transition into a part-time role. If you can stand to keep me around . . ."

"Are you kidding? That goes without saying, Tom. You're the heart and soul of this firm."

"All good things come to an end, my friend. I've loved being at the helm of the firm. We've weathered recessions, grown from being a sole practitioner to where we are today. We survived going paperless and even kept up pretty well with all the new technology. In spite of all the changes and challenges, we've always produced a superior work product. But that's just not enough anymore."

I was uneasy, and he must have seen it. He added, "Look, don't think for a minute I'm stepping down because I feel pressured to do so. I'm doing it because it's in the best interest of the firm. It's the right move at the right time."

"I won't kid you. I can't pretend I'm not a little nervous about it."

"I'd be concerned if you weren't, but I know you can handle it. You have so many great ideas, and you'll finally get to follow through on that advisory training you went to a couple years ago. What was that called?"

"Level 5 Service."

"Right. Okay, Mr. Level 5, it's time to go live! I'll have my office cleared out by the end of the week so you can move in. I'll take Mark's old office."

I was speechless. Tom was quiet for a moment, too.

"Not to sound too paternal, but I'm very proud of you, Bennie. You've been like a son to me in so many ways. You've been here through thick and thin, and I genuinely look forward to watching you in action. And don't worry about push-back from Howard or Newt," he said, chuckling knowingly. "They're scared to death there won't be a buyout for them in a couple of years when they're ready to retire. They *know* we need to shift gears and head in a new direction. I think Sharon is already celebrating. You should call her."

A warm hug and smile from Tom sealed the deal. As I watched him gather up his coffee and head down the hall to his office, I noticed a slight bounce in his step. His face seemed brighter than it had in a very long time.

Sitting in the parking lot, I punched in the number. It took two attempts to get through; I figured she was pulling over. She'd seen too many accidents due to cell phone use, and she never spoke while driving. "Sharon, it's Bennie. Sorry I didn't get back to you sooner. We've had family over –"

Sharon interrupted, "Oh, shut up already. Congratulations!!! It's about time. I wondered how long it would take before this would happen. I just want you to know I've got your back 100%. Anything you need, I'm there." She was speaking loudly into the phone. I could hear the occasional car drive by in the background.

"Thanks, your support means a lot to me. I just met with Tom, and it hasn't quite sunk in. I'm not sure how I feel right now. I've been waiting a long time for this, and yet, now that it's here . . ." I searched for the right words and came up blank.

"You can do this, Bennie. You'll be great. It's just the shot in the arm the team needs. There were some very unhappy faces around the office Friday afternoon, hearing Mark and Katie had left. I think Mark and Katie were just the beginning. I wouldn't be surprised if others are sprucing up their résumés as we speak."

"I wondered about that, too. Who do you think?"

"Not today, my friend. We're not having *that* discussion right now. Today is about celebrating. Have you told Anna yet?"

"No, not yet. I haven't had a chance. I need to get home, spend some time with her and the kids. I'll need their support, too."

"What are you waiting for? Hang up the phone and get to it. Goodbye, Fearless Leader!" I pictured her jumping back on her bike and heading down the road.

Sharon is the most unlikely accountant you can imagine. It's as if she steps into a phone booth and comes out a different person when she comes to work each day – from leather duds to leather briefcase. By day she's an accountant, but the rest of the time, she's a Harley riding, road tripping, Sturgis loving fanatic. She doesn't give up much about her personal life, except the one picture in her office with her in full leather gear on her Harley.

On the surface, she's pretty laid back, but she's not afraid to speak up when the situation calls for it. In the past, she'd had run-ins with Howard and Newt. Although all three of them were highly skilled at the technical aspects of their jobs, their styles were very different. More than once, Tom has had to mediate between them. It was reassuring to know I could count on her as well as Tom to support me with moving the firm forward.

It's all about perspective . . .

Many years ago, a large shoe company sent two sales representatives out to different parts of the Australian outback to see if they could drum up some business among the Aborigines. Sometime later, the company received telegrams from both agents.

The first said, "No business here . . . natives don't wear shoes."

The second one said, "Great opportunity here . . . natives don't wear shoes!"

John M. Capozzi

Balance

I drove home a little more slowly than usual, stopping to buy some flowers for Anna. The looming demands on my time and energy would put a real strain on the family. My new mantra would have to be "balance." In the 20 minutes it took to get from the office to the house, I could feel a swell of excitement in my gut or maybe it was butterflies. Likely both. Either way, the wheels were already in motion. I, too, felt a little bounce in my step.

"Honey, I'm home!"

"We're in the kitchen."

"Daddy, Daddy! Come see our pretty toes!" cried Susie.

As I came around the corner toward the kitchen, it smelled like a beauty salon. "Pedicures for all" seemed to be the activity of the day.

Susie, in her sweet 4-year-old voice, said, "It's paw day!"

"I see that and smell it, too. Is everyone having fun on spa day?"

"Oh yes, Daddy." Caroline pointed at her feet. "I'm painting every one of my toes a different color. How about you, Daddy, can I paint your toes?"

"Oh, maybe next time."

Anna quietly asked, "How did it go?"

"Better than I imagined."

"Do tell."

"How do you like the sound of Bennett Stewart, Managing

Partner?"

Caroline jumped right in and said it sounded ridiculous. "You're Bennie Stewart, not Bennett, Daddy!"

Nomi, Karen, Anna, and I all laughed at Caroline's take on my big announcement.

"Indeed, I am Bennie Stewart. But now that I'm Managing Partner maybe I should upgrade my name to something a bit more formal, like Bennett."

My mom spoke up, "Not on your life! It took me ten years to get used to Bennie. Don't you dare go and try to be someone you aren't!"

Spa day was winding down. Nomi herded the girls upstairs for some quiet time. Karen got busy cleaning up the spa mess so they could start on dinner. "I've got this, Anna. You two take a few minutes before the boys get back."

With an appreciative smile to her sister, taking me by the hand Anna ushered me out to the patio. She'd somehow managed to put a couple of cold beers in her apron pocket without me even noticing. "We'll open the champagne another day. For now, these will have to do."

"I have something for you, too." I ran back in the house and grabbed the flowers I'd left in the foyer.

"For you, my love; a little token of my affection and gratitude in advance."

"In advance?"

"I'll need a lot of patience and support from you over the next few months while we make the transition. I guess I'm thanking you *and* apologizing for it in advance."

"Although you never need to ask for it, it's nice that you don't take it for granted either. You're most welcome, and thanks for the gorgeous flowers."

The cold beer tasted especially wonderful in that moment. We sipped, and Anna asked the same question she'd posed to me on Friday night.

"With the chance to start fresh, what are you going to do differently?

My mind was brimming with ideas, fears, concerns, and excitement, the whole gamut of emotion.

"I'm not even sure where to start, Anna. There's so much I've been wanting to do, and now I get to do it. My mind is racing. I'm not sure I really know how to answer that question."

In typical Anna fashion, she said, "Let me reframe the question, it's a year from now, and we're celebrating a year of accomplishments with a special bottle of champagne. What did you accomplish?"

This was a technique Anna and I had used for much of our life planning activities over the years. We weren't always sure *how* we were going to accomplish something, so we focused on what our life would look or feel like *when* we got to the other side of *how*. This "future-framing" started from something my Mom said to me after my dad died. I was struggling with how to go on without him, and Mom said, "Focus on what you want for your future and leave the *how* for the universe to answer." That advice helped me stay focused on positive feelings and not get mired down in the sadness or details of the day.

I asked Anna, "Is it a sparkling cider kind of celebration or a fancy champagne celebration?"

"I think you're overdue for a *real* celebration. Think big." She gave me a minute to think it over, then asked, "So, what are we celebrating?"

"Well, when you put it like that . . .

"We're celebrating a waiting list of great businesses that want to work with our firm.
We're celebrating increasing our revenues by 30%.
We're celebrating that our clients' businesses are thriving.
We're celebrating admitting two new partners to the firm, with more right behind them on a clearly defined partner development track.
We're celebrating having the very best talent available, with more knocking on our door every day.
We're celebrating a 50/50 ratio of compliance to advisory services.
And, we're celebrating that I was able to make all this happen without compromising our family time in the process.

"*That* is what we're celebrating!" I'd said it all with honest enthusiasm and all the confidence that I could muster, which was easier now that I'd talked things over with Anna.

Anna smiled broadly, kissed me on the cheek, then replied, "Remember, Bennie, the only thing standing between where you are right now and where you want to take the firm is your resolve. You have my complete support. Think of it as payback for all the support you gave me during grad school."

Hail, Hail

"Hail, hail, the gang's all here!" Nomi's voice sang out.

Chaos, the kind we all love, ensued. Apparently, Karen had called Josh on his way back from miniature golf. He had two bottles of decent – but not fancy – champagne in hand as he came through the kitchen door onto the patio. Karen followed close behind with glasses. Nomi set the kids up with sparkling cider and paper cups.

Josh led the toast, "Cheers to Bennie! Congratulations to you on stepping up as Managing Partner! And just so you know, Bennie, about our conversation last night. As you raise your glass to this new position, I'm raising my expectations of the firm, have you got that?"

"Got it."

Later, with everyone gone and the kids in bed, there was time for me to consider what Josh had said. The real question was, "Got what?" What expectations? And what to do first? As we crawled into bed that night, Anna asked what I was thinking about. I told her I was struggling with what to do first.

"*What* may not be the right place to start," she said quietly.

"What do you mean?"

"Maybe the better place to start is *why*? Remember that TED Talk video you shared with me a couple years ago? What was that speaker's name?"

I was always amazed by how tuned in Anna was. "Simon Sinek. How do you remember so much of what I share with you?"

"I could tell you I remember *everything*, but that would be a lie. But, that video, and that training when you were first exposed to it, lit a fire in you I hadn't seen in a long time. I've been waiting for it to burn brightly again."

She was right and I knew it. *Why* was the question filling my thoughts as I drifted off to sleep. Tomorrow was the first day of the rest of my life; it was at once daunting and exhilarating.

Why was important, but the first order of business on Monday was to tell the team. What would I say to them that would instill confidence, inspire them, and dispel any rumors that might be circulating?

I also kept thinking that maybe it wasn't too late to get Katie and Mark back on board. And damn it, I wasn't going to let Jack Marshall go without a fight. I had some very important tasks ahead of me.

The alarm went off and I jumped into the shower. Anna was already busy getting the kids going and fixing lunches by the time I got downstairs. She'd fixed me a "leftovers lunch" out of all the food from the weekend. On my way to the office, I had to drop Chris off at school. Chris and I scarfed down a little breakfast before we headed for the door.

"Slow down, wait just a minute, Mr. Managing Partner. Where's my hug and kiss?" Chris smiled and rolled his eyes at us having a quick moment. He got a peck on the cheek from his mom, as well.

On the way to school, Chris mused how he hoped someday he'd find a woman as great as his mom. I told him he'd indeed be blessed if he lucked out like I had.

"Dad, are you excited about what's about to happen today?"

"I'm excited, but I'm also nervous. There's a lot riding on me to get this right."

"Dad, something Coach always says might help. 'There's no I in TEAM.' Maybe you should think of it that way, that there's a lot riding on everyone to get it right. No one ever wins or loses the game all by themselves."

"How did you get so smart? Great advice. You're right, it isn't all about me. It's about everyone's future. We succeed or fail together, as a team."

As we were pulling into the school parking lot, Chris added even more.

"Maybe you should think of yourself as a coach rather than a managing partner. Coach always says that he can only get us so far with skills and drills. The decisions we make on the field are the real test of our abilities."

"Skills and drills, huh?"

"Yup, skills and drills. Love you, Dad. Have a great day!"

In Aristotelian terms, the good leader must have ethos, pathos and logos. The ethos is his moral character, the source of his (or her) ability to persuade. The pathos is his ability to touch feelings to move people emotionally. The logos is his ability to give solid reasons for an action, to move people intellectually.

Mortimer Jerome Adler

Monday

My mental checklist was growing by the minute. I'd left the office on Friday feeling pretty discouraged and uncertain. But then, yesterday, I'd realized a lifelong dream: Tom was giving me the chance to lead the firm *my way*. All of this had transpired in less than 48 hours.

We give our folks flextime – the ability to shift their hours to fit their personal needs – so it was pretty quiet when I came in through the back door at 7:30 a.m. The office didn't really start humming until 9:00 a.m.

I ducked into my office and closed the door. Sighing deeply, I sat down in the same chair I'd sat in forever. Same desk, same view, same stack of client files waiting for my attention.

"Clients!" I said aloud. What was I going to do with all my client responsibilities? As the firm had grown, I'd watched Tom cut back on his client load over time. He would say, "The firm is my client."

I realized I didn't have the luxury of time. I was going to have to do some major surgery on my client list to give the firm the attention it deserved. I would need a lot of help, and losing Mark and Katie was just not an option. I had to get them back.

Dear Mark and Katie,

Thank you both for your e-mail over the weekend. I understand your frustrations, but much has changed since you gave notice on Thursday. I MUST SEE YOU BOTH TODAY! Can we meet for lunch at The Grill on 4th at noon? I'll make the reservation.

Bennie

Less than five minutes passed when I got a reply from Mark.

Bennie,

Yes, we can meet for lunch. Are you ready to jump in with us? Hope so.

Mark (and Katie)

Next order of business: Jack Marshall.

Jack,

You've been a great client over the years. Clearly, we haven't held up our end of the bargain. I understand why you told Tom about your plans to move your business elsewhere. May I ask a favor?

Before you head in that direction, I'd like to meet with you.

No hard sell, and that's a promise. I think I know what was missing from the relationship, and I'd like the chance to talk with you about how things will be different going forward. I think you'll like what you hear.

Can you do breakfast tomorrow morning? I'll come by at 7a.m. with some bagels and coffee. How do you take yours?

Bennie

Jack is an early riser like me and has always preferred a breakfast meeting over lunch. He must have been sitting in his office because within three minutes my phone rang.

"Bennie, it's Jack. I'm glad I caught you. It was a hard conversation with Tom last week, without a chance to properly thank you for your service over the years. I appreciate the offer of breakfast, but I'm not sure anything you could say would change my mind," he said.

"Maybe, but I'd still like the chance to personally share my vision for the future of our firm, and what that means for our clients. As of today – the announcement is coming later so please keep this under wraps – I'm the new managing partner."

"Wow . . . please don't tell me my conversation with Tom got him fired."

"No, of course not!" I said, trying to keep my tone lighthearted. "We don't fire partners. This transition has been in progress for some time now," a small white lie. "And it's not about the performance of any one person. We all win or lose together," I added, silently thanking Chris. "Look, I know there have been disappointments in recent years. I'd like to understand, from your perspective, how we can do things better from now on."

I waited for Jack to push back. He didn't. Instead, in a very matter of fact tone he said, "Venti Americana, black."

"Great, I'll see you then."

But the customer was clearly not finished ordering, "Wait, onion bagel with salmon cream cheese."

"Anything else?"

"Nope, that'll do it. See you in the morning."

I was beginning to feel hopeful about rewinding the clock to before things unraveled. My optimism was quickly tempered by the reality that my vision had to be clear enough, and strong enough, to inspire Mark, Katie, and Jack to give us another chance. Even more important than the vision, I wondered if I had the political capital to move the firm forward in this new direction.

A knock on my door signaled the end of my quiet thinking time. It was time for some action.

"Come in."

It was Margaret Sullivan, our office manager. "Good morning, Bennie. If it's not a bad time, may I have a few minutes?"

I wasn't sure how much Margaret did or didn't know, but since she was going to be my right hand in running the firm, I figured there was no time like the present.

"Of course, always. As a matter of fact, I'm glad you popped in. We have big things, important things, to discuss."

In a very serious voice, Margaret flatly stated, "My turn first, Bennie. Tom called me last night to give me a heads up. I've worked with Tom for 23 years, starting out as a file clerk – if you remember those days – moving on to admin support, then office manager. He's the most generous, supportive person I've ever had the pleasure to work for. I'm just –"

A jolt of panic ran up my spine. "Oh no, not you, too! Are you upset about Tom stepping down? Are you giving notice?"

With a twinkle in her eye, the sternness around her mouth softening, she said, "Of course, not, Bennie. I've worked with you for 20 of those 23 years. I've watched you grow from a junior to become a great mentor and leader. I've already had a taste of working with you, when Tom was going through prostate cancer and out of the office for six weeks. I also know this transition has been informally floating out there for years. I'm here to say, I'm glad it finally happened, and I couldn't be happier."

"Whew, that's a relief. If you were walking out the door, I'd probably have to follow you. I *know*, with absolute certainty, that I cannot move the firm forward without you."

Margaret smiled. She seemed to appreciate the compliment, but didn't dwell on it. "Tom isn't well. I'm not sure if it's just burnout or something worse, but I've watched him decline this past year. He's been spread so thin . . . I've tried – on many occasions, without success – to get him to move more administrative duties to me. For the health of the firm, and Tom's health in particular, the timing of this transition couldn't be better. I take that back, a couple years ago would have been even better. Maybe we wouldn't have lost Mark and Katie or Star Industries."

"Well, have faith. All may not be lost on either front. I have a lunch meeting with Mark and Katie at The Grill at noon and breakfast with Jack at seven tomorrow."

Beaming a wide smile and noting the bag on my desk, she asked, "Shall I put your lunch in the fridge? Will you be needing a reservation for lunch?"

"Thank you, yes. As for the reservation –"

"The Grill, noon, party of three. I'll ask for a booth; you'll want some privacy," she said, finishing my sentence. It was almost daunting to have someone so efficient supporting me.

"One more thing, Margaret. Don't let Tom get too carried away with moving out of his office. Distract him for a few hours until I get back from lunch. I'm hoping Mark's office will no longer be available."

"But if he comes back – and I hope he does – aren't you moving into Tom's office?"

"I'm not going anywhere. I like my office. Tom thinks I need the prestige of the big corner office, but that doesn't really matter to me."

Margaret grinned, she seemed to be enjoying this. "If it's okay with you, I might hold off on telling Tom. He's already spent a few hours cleaning and organizing. I haven't seen space on his credenza in years. We'll let him keep going, okay? I promise, I'll stop him if I catch him wheeling his chair down the hall." Margaret didn't wait for my answer. If there was one thing you could say about her, it was that she knew how to make things happen.

And she was on a roll. "Tom mentioned you'd be gathering the team today for the announcement. What time shall I pull everyone together? We've got a couple people in the field I need to reach."

"Let's say 4 p.m. That should give me time after getting back from lunch."

"Done," she said, and she meant it. I knew I could count on her to follow-through on anything and everything I asked of her. I could also count on her to push back when her plate was full or if she didn't agree with something.

I always wondered why Tom didn't give her more responsibilities. I resolved not to underutilize her talents. My survival – and keeping a healthy balance with my home and work life – depended on it.

I walked over to Tom's office. It looked as if a bomb had gone off.

"Good morning. How's it going?" I asked.

"I'm pretty excited to tell you the truth. I already feel like a new man. Maybe I should have done this years ago. Connie is so excited that she's already scouring Internet listings for Montana real estate."

"Are you moving? You promised to be here to help with the transition."

I had a silent panic attack. I tried not to let it show, but I still had mixed feelings about the transition. Part of me was excited about taking the helm. The other part was already trying to imagine what it would be like without Tom around. My mom never remarried after my dad passed away. I was lucky enough to have some good mentors over the years, but it wasn't until I started working alongside Tom that some of the ache from missing my dad began to subside. This day was bittersweet. Yes, I was realizing a dream, but I was also watching my surrogate father preparing for the next phase of his life, a phase that didn't include being a regular fixture in mine.

"I used to think I would work until the day I died, but Connie has a different agenda. I don't want you to worry; we're not moving anytime soon. But that's not going to stop Connie from looking. We've always talked about a second home, but it wasn't practical with me taking so little time off. Now it is."

"Okay with you if I schedule the partner meeting for 10am?" I asked.

"The rest of the team may not know it yet, but you're in charge. If you're asking if my schedule is clear, the answer is yes." Surveying the room, he said, "I welcome the interruption. This clean up might take me a bit longer than I thought . . . quite a few piles to wade through."

I thought about my conversation with Margaret. Maybe we shouldn't slow him down. A few more hours – or days – made a lot of sense.

I popped my head in on Margaret. "Please ask the partners to join me in the conference room at 10 a.m. Short notice, I know, but I need their approval on something before I go to lunch."

"Done."

I took a deep breath approaching the conference room. There they were, settled in at 10, sharp. All except Howard, who has never been on time a day in his life. Never terribly late, but he was never on time, either.

An old memory hit me. My dad arranged my first summer job when I was 10 years old. It was just sweeping, stocking, and miscellaneous errands at his client's hardware store. I looked at it as spending money; Dad saw it as the start of my college fund. He felt it was important that I be invested in my future and gain a strong work ethic from an early age. Looking back, I don't think I had a choice in the matter.

At first, I was excited to get to my job every morning at 7:30a.m., but after the first couple weeks, the novelty wore off. My friends were home all summer with nothing to do – except sleep in and tease me about having to get up and go to work every day.

One morning, I overslept and Dad had to wake me up. Running late, Dad offered to drive me. He wasn't driving me to work because he wanted to help me out: one of his "teaching moments" had just presented itself.

From time to time, my friends talked about getting the "living daylights" beaten out of them for screwing up. Although my father never laid a hand on me, I sometimes wished for that rather than his famous tongue lashings. They were precious "teaching gems", and now, as a parent, I marvel at how he always kept his cool. By the time he was done "talking," you were pummeled into intellectual and emotional submission.

"Bennett," he said (I hadn't changed my name yet), "being a few minutes late for a job may not seem like a big deal. Sweeping floors and running errands may not feel like the most important job in the world, but that's not your call. When Mr. Harmon hired you for the summer, he made a commitment: a commitment to organize his day around making sure you had tasks to complete. He made a financial commitment, too, taking money out of his pocket to pay you for the summer. In exchange, you made commitments to him. You committed to work hard to earn your pay, to be honest and trustworthy. You also committed to represent him as an ambassador in the store. When people are counting on you, it's disrespectful to waste their time by being late."

"You're right, Dad, but I won't be late now; you're dropping me off."

"True, but it's the last time I'll rescue you when you screw up this way. I'm doing this because Mr. Harmon is a good client and close friend. He did me a favor, giving you a job at your age and turning down older boys who wanted it. He promised me that he'd watch over you and give you a good first work experience, and I'll do the same for his son, George, when he turns ten."

Dad continued, "My first boss was not as forgiving as Mr. Harmon. He had a little sign over the time clock that read:

> **Early = On Time**
> **On Time = Late**
> **Late = Fired**

Dad explained, "If you're early, you will be at your station and ready to begin work at the appointed time. If you're on time, you're late because you'll need a few minutes to clock in and get ready to do the work you were hired to do. And if you're late, you're fired. Got it?"

"Yes, I've got it."

I worked for Mr. Harmon that summer and the next several, through high school. When my dad passed away, Mr. Harmon watched over me. He promoted me to cashier at 14. At 16, he let me work around my sports and after school activities. His flexibility resulted in me doing bookkeeping for him: closing out the day's receipts, inventory management, even the bank reconciliations. Turns out I had a good head for numbers, but I might not have known that if Mr. Harmon hadn't given me that responsibility and the opportunity. He's the reason I decided to go into accounting. Working in a small business also helped me understand what a lot of my clients deal with on a daily basis.

Mr. Harmon didn't just watch over me at work. He watched over our home, too. He made sure our house stayed in good repair and helped my mom with any maintenance issues that arose. He taught me how to repair things, how to use power tools, and not to fear home improvement projects. He was a real jack-of-all-trades, and I learned a lot from him, knowledge that has served me well with my own home. We spent many Thanksgivings with his family over the years. By the time his son George turned ten, my dad was already gone. I can't help but think of what a great mentor my dad would have been for George.

While we waited for Howard, we passed the time talking about the weather, Friday night football game, and other trivial stuff. Howard rushed in looking at his watch. He was 13 minutes late. Not bad by his standards, but clearly he'd wasted everyone's time by keeping us waiting.

Granted, he'd been given short notice of the meeting, but this was a pattern that set the tone for others in the office. Tom tolerated it, but I knew it frustrated him. It also frustrated the team when they were left waiting on Howard for various reasons. I planned to have a conversation with him, but not today.

I waited for Tom to get us started with a formal announcement about the transition, but he was quiet.

So I prompted him, "Tom, anything you want to say to start us off?"

"Howard, Newt, Sharon, I'd like to introduce you to our new managing partner. Take it away, Bennie."

I guess I was expecting something more significant to mark the moment. It wasn't forthcoming. Just as well, given the issues we were facing.

Sensing the awkwardness, Sharon raised her coffee mug and said, "Cheers! Here's to so many great years of leadership with Tom at the helm and to many more with Bennie, our new fearless leader."

That was the second time in two days she had referred to me as a fearless leader. I sure wasn't feeling fearless. I wasn't sure if Sharon was teasing or encouraging me; she had a dry wit that often left me wondering if I had missed her meaning.

"Cheers!" echoed Tom. Howard and Newt raised their mugs, but I wondered about their enthusiasm or lack thereof. Sharon shot me a wry smile.

They all turned toward me and waited.

"First, thanks to all of you for your confidence in my ability to step into Tom's shoes. They're big shoes to fill, and I'll do my very best to wear them well."

Tom interrupted, "Bennie, thank *you* for your kind words, but I sure hope you don't step into my shoes. I'm still wearing oxfords. You'll need running shoes to manage the changes ahead. It's not that we're that far behind our peers, in fact I think we are right on par, but that's not necessarily good news. I don't want us to be on par, I'd like to think we could move ahead of other firms by addressing a broader range of client needs. I'm not even sure business owners know what they need because so much is changing so fast in their world, but we have an opportunity to take the lead and help them navigate through those changes. I want everyone to hear me on this. Bennie will do things differently than I did. He won't follow conventions, and he'll probably scare the hell out of us with some of his radical ideas, but those radical ideas will ensure the future of the firm. Change is hard, and I know we have big challenges ahead, but if we stick together, we can break out of old patterns and build a lasting legacy for others to follow in *our* shoes. Bennie is the perfect leader to move this firm forward."

That was the speech I'd been waiting for. Tom had passed the baton. Now it was my turn to grab hold and run with it.

With the conceptual baton in hand, I began. "I've thought about this moment for a long time but in truth, my fantasies of what I thought I'd say don't measure up with what is needed at this point in time.

"When we headed home on Friday, we were charged to come back together today to essentially address three problems:

1) How do we build revenues?
2) How do we keep clients happy?
3) How do we keep the team happy?

"Before I share my thoughts, I'm wondering what you came up with."

Newt started. "I think we should look at raising our fees to cover some of the shortfall. We need to hire a recruiter to look for some top end talent to replace Mark and Katie."

As he was talking, I realized we needed one more person in the room.

"Excuse me, Newt, please hold that thought. I'll be right back."

Scooting down the hallway, I knew I'd left some puzzled faces behind.

"Margaret, please join us for the partners meeting. I need you."

By the look on her face, I might have asked her to jump off the roof.

"Do you need me to bring you something?"

"Just bring yourself, and to be clear, I want you at every one of these meetings from here on out."

Margaret hesitated, and I knew why. When Tom was out for several weeks recovering from prostate surgery, I'd asked Margaret to sit in on a partner meeting. Howard was not pleased, and he lacked the emotional intelligence to take the conversation off-line. Instead, he objected profusely about having a non-partner at the partner meeting. It embarrassed Margaret. It infuriated me, but I wasn't strong enough then to stand up to Howard. I think he resented me because Tom put me in charge instead of him. From Tom's perspective, it made all the sense in the world since I would be stepping into his role someday. From Howard's perspective, his seniority made him the logical choice. Howard apologized weeks later but only after Tom reamed him up one side and down the other when he found out what had happened. Since then Howard has been very cautious around Margaret. The Margaret I knew was always comfortable in her own skin so it was uncharacteristic for her to be sheepish.

"Are you sure about this?" She asked.

"Absolutely."

She rose slowly at first, then grabbed her pad, a pen, and marched down the hall and joined us like she'd done it hundreds of times before.

When Margaret entered the room, Sharon and Tom smiled. Newt looked anxious. Howard looked at me, and I looked right back at him. He blinked first. *I win,* I thought to myself and felt a small smile start to form. I caught a glimpse of Sharon, and she appeared to be holding back a smile as well.

After one particularly nasty partner meeting when Howard and Newt were on a rant about compensation, Sharon teasingly offered to talk to one of her biker friends about *taking care* of Howard and Newt. I know she was kidding, at least I hope so. You never know with Sharon. There's more to her than meets the eye. One thing's for sure, she's in my corner if for no other reason than to antagonize Howard and Newt. I could tell she was feeling the power shift in the room as much as I was.

"From here on out, these meetings will include the entire leadership team unless otherwise specified." I turned to Newt.

"Now where were we? Ah, Newt, you were sharing some ideas for how we can address the current situation. Your first idea was raising fees. The second was hiring a recruiter to replace Mark and Katie. Have I got that right? Please continue."

I made some notes.

"I was also thinking that we could each join a board of directors to do some prospecting for new clients. That's about as far as I got," Newt said.

"Thanks, Newt. Howard, how about you? Any ideas?"

"I was thinking that we could start asking for more referrals. We could also get the team out prospecting more. Maybe have each of them come up with their own marketing plan and hold them accountable to it."

"Okay, any others?"

Sharon waited briefly before diplomatically jumping in. "Those are some pretty tried and true ideas that might help replace the lost revenue, but long term it may not be enough. Right now we're like a leaking bath tub: we keep filling it up with clients, but until we figure out how to service them better, they'll continue leaking out the bottom."

"Is there an idea in there, Sharon?"

"Sure. We might want to consider interviewing our clients to figure out what they really want from us. Everybody talks about doing advisory work, but what does that really mean? Perhaps our clients can help us narrow the focus of our efforts. Along those same lines, I think we should revisit that Level 5 Service training material from a couple years ago. I was also thinking that the team probably should be in on this discussion."

Margaret smiled at that. "I like what Sharon just said. The team is as concerned as we are with the recent developments. We need to quash their fears by including them in this dialogue. Plus, many of them understand social media and can extend our reach considerably if we allow them to use that knowledge to help grow the firm. Tom, we've had this discussion before. I know your concerns about opening the Internet floodgates, but I have to tell you, when I go to firm administrator conferences, we're pretty far behind what many other firms are doing."

Everyone looked at Tom waiting for some push back. There wasn't any.

Tom seized the moment. "Margaret, you're right. It's time to look at the firm from a whole new perspective. I shied away from social media because I don't really understand it, but that's no longer a good reason. I'll leave that decision up to Bennie and the rest of you."

Sharon looked at me and said, "Okay, Bennie, what about your ideas?"

"I have a lot of them, some practical, some wild and even a little crazy. Too many to lay out on the table today, but I do have two steps I am going to take immediately that might help turn this trend around sooner rather than later.

"First, I've scheduled a breakfast with Jack Marshall tomorrow morning to see if I can convince him to give us another chance. Second, I've been in touch with Mark and Katie. We're having lunch at noon. My hope is to get them back on board by day's end. If I can get them to come back, I am going to have them lead the Level 5 Service launch starting ASAP. Even if they don't come back, Sharon, you and I will be the ones to make that happen."

Newt asked, "Do you really think it's wise to allow Mark and Katie back in the firm? Doesn't it set a bad precedent?"

"Precedent? The precedent we don't want to set is that our managers have to leave to start their own practices because we're stuck in our old ways! I'm not concerned about them coming back to work tomorrow. I know with certainty we could look forever and never find two managers as skilled and dedicated to this firm as they are."

Newt responded, "Dedicated? What about loyal? In my book, they failed the loyalty test."

It was everything I could do to keep my cool. I'd heard comments like this from Newt and Howard for years. I'd ignored them for the most part, but today was different. This was Katie and Mark he was disparaging; they deserved more respect.

"Don't take this the wrong way, Newt, but I think *we* failed the loyalty test. We're the ones who didn't follow through on our commitment to lay out a path to partnership for the two of them. We sent them off to advisory skills training but didn't free up any time for them to master their new skills. Not to mention, we were so internally focused we ignored their progressive ideas about *proactively* helping our clients navigate the recession."

Newt squirmed a bit but didn't say anything. I looked over at Tom for his reaction; he gave me a slight nod and wink to continue.

"Here's what I'm more concerned about: just imagine for a moment I get Mark, Katie, and Jack back on board, and we drop the ball again. I doubt our reputation could take a hit like that in this community. It's a small town, and people talk. Not that Mark or Katie would ever disparage the firm, but their exodus sends its own message, and not just to the community, but to our entire team and clients. I can promise you every one of them pondered their future at this firm over the weekend. It's up to *us* to demonstrate our loyalty to *them*. It's far easier to replace a lost client, even one as big as Star Industries, than to replace great talent."

"Bravo!" Sharon could hardly contain herself. "No offense, Tom, but I've been waiting a long time to hear someone in this firm put our people first. Not that you didn't care, but the message that 'clients come first' can't come at the cost of our people."

"No offense taken, Sharon. Top talent wasn't so hard to come by when we were first building the firm, but over the past few years it's gotten a lot harder to find quality people. The rules of the game have changed, and so must we," Tom answered, and I could tell he really meant it.

Looking at my watch, I had to be on the road in 20 minutes to make lunch with Mark and Katie.

"I wish we had days to really dig into these topics, but for now, thank you for your input, I really appreciate it. Right now, I need to turn a lunch date into a happy marriage: part of what I want to discuss with Mark and Katie is their timeline for partnership. Tom, I know you had some thoughts when we covered this at the retreat."

Tom said, "We discussed potentially making them associate partners for a year, a probationary period with clearly defined objectives to evaluate their performance. Is that what you were referring to?"

"That's what I remembered, too. Are you all comfortable with me putting that on the table today? I know we have a lot of details to backfill on this, but I don't want to go into this meeting empty handed. Promises won't cut it; they know us too well. They've watched us fiddle around with things but never fully implement. I want to prove to them that we're serious about keeping them on board. Any objections?"

There were nods from everyone indicating I had the go ahead.

"Margaret, is everything set for the meeting today?"

"Yes, I got a hold of everyone. We'll all be gathered at 4 p.m."

"Great. Thank you again for your support. I've thought about this day for many years. In my wildest dreams, it didn't look like this, but sometimes it takes some pain to create the focus and urgency needed to move things in a new direction. I am going to need your patience and support as we move the firm forward in the coming weeks. I may move pretty fast on some things; I promise I will do my best to keep you informed on important issues. At the same time, I won't be checking in with you on all the details along the way. Now more than ever, our leadership team needs to stick together with a unified voice. Agreed?" It wasn't really a question. I didn't wait for a response. In fact, I didn't want to give Howard or Newt the chance to speak. I had a feeling I would have to have a quiet conversation with each of them, separately. As much as Tom reassured me they were on board, I wasn't convinced.

"I need to head out. I'll see everyone at 4."

As I headed down the hallway Margaret accompanied me in lock step.

"Do you need me to do anything special while you're at lunch?"

"No. I mean, yes. Would you please get me the current home address and phone numbers of each employee. I'd also like to sit down with you in the next few days to have you brief me on some of the vital statistics on everyone: spouses' and kids' names and ages, hobbies and interests, birthdays, performance issues, et cetera. Maybe you could start gathering all that together for me?"

"Done. Good luck at lunch. By the way, Mark's wife is Sue, and Katie's husband is Chris. Mark and Sue put off trying for kids because of this new venture; some stability might go a long way with him. Katie and Chris are all about a flexible lifestyle, and they're very active in sports."

Margaret had her finger on the pulse of the firm like no one else. Employees came to her with their issues; as the de facto HR Director, she knew everything about everyone. She probably knew about Mark and Katie's decision even before they sat down with Tom on Thursday.

Inviting Margaret to the meeting was the right thing to do. She belonged in that room as much as the rest of us. It felt good to assert some authority especially given the history between Howard and Margaret. I think it made a difference to her, too. She'd gone from supporting me as Tom's replacement to being my right arm in less than a day.

On the way to the restaurant, I was thinking about what Sharon had said about putting the team first. My dad often told the story about a veterinarian client he had. It was timelier than ever. The vet noticed that his team was grumbling about the rudeness of some of their clients. He decided that part of the team's Christmas bonus that year would be that he would allow them to fire two clients each. With ten employees, he sweated over the thought of potentially firing 20 clients, but to his delight the team decided to meet together and review the entire client list. In the end, they nominated just four clients for dismissal.

The vet said that two of the clients came as no surprise to him. The other two did. He noted that although those clients had been polite with him they had been rude to his staff. He immediately fired the four clients. In doing so, it sent a clear message to the team: you're more important to the practice than any individual client we serve. From that point forward, the team was quick to let the vet know about clients that routinely failed the respect and courtesy test.

With this simple act of eliminating nuisance clients from the practice, the vet communicated volumes about his loyalty to the team. The moral of the story: no one client is more important to the firm than the happiness of the team.

Taking that thought a bit further, I've always thought we spent too much time dealing with nuisance clients that suck the life out of the team, at the expense of being available to help good clients – the starving crowd. As crazy as it sounds, especially given the recent loss of two big clients, I couldn't wait to start trimming the deadwood off our client list, a topic many times visited but never fully implemented by the partner group.

If you just work for money, you'll never make it, but if you love what you're doing . . . success will be yours.

Ray Kroc

What's On the Menu?

I arrived at the restaurant with a few minutes to spare. Mark and Katie were already seated, with beverages.

"Hi guys. Thanks for agreeing to meet today."

"Of course, Bennie," Katie said, "We hoped you would be in touch. Should we order before we dive into this discussion?"

Ordering gave me time to gather my thoughts. With that out of the way, I was ready, and began.

"Okay, no ill feelings. That said, I wish you'd come to me, first."

Mark replied, "Would it have made a difference? You and I had conversations about a partnership path more times than I can count. We know you weren't the one making the final decisions and didn't want to burden you with an issue you had no control over."

"A lot has happened since you left on Thursday. Sometimes it takes a wakeup call like losing the two of you before people are willing to change. As of this morning, I'm Managing Partner, and I now have the power to make changes."

I paused for effect. I wanted to see how they would react to the news. They were both quiet.

"What do you think of that?"

Katie went first. "Congratulations, Bennie. You'll do a great job." She paused, as if searching for the right words, then asked, "How's Tom with all this?"

"He's fine. It was his idea to step aside. For all intents and purposes, it was a done deal, at least in his mind. I always wondered when and how the transition would come about. I never expected it to come so swiftly, but here we are and now I get to call the shots."

Mark asked, "What does this mean for the firm? Do you expect things to change much, or will you get a lot of pushback from the other partners?"

"So far, everyone seems willing to ride the Bennie train. I just have to figure out where I'm going. One thing is for sure: I don't want this train leaving the station without the two of you. I need you two back on board."

Scratching his head, Mark replied, "Honestly, Bennie, we thought you asked us out to lunch to talk about joining us. It never occurred to us that you would be asking us to come back. I'm a bit shocked."

Katie sat up straight. "Bennie, I'm not interested in going back in time. I spent the weekend dreaming about doing meaningful work with clients. I pulled out my manual from the Level 5 Service training and got my head wrapped around what our service offerings are going to look like. Mark and I have been talking about making this move for months. Our spouses are on board. I'm not sure the Thomas & Perish or Perish & Thomas train can be stopped now. Or that I *want* to stop it."

This was going to be harder than I realized. I hadn't really bargained for how invested they were in an alternate future. I should have expected it. Mark and Katie are thoughtful and deliberate people. They never would have embarked on this new venture without a lot of soul searching and planning.

"I am prepared to offer you both a 10% raise and associate partnership right this minute."

Katie was quick to respond, "Wow, Bennie. That's very kind of you."

"Kind is not the response I was hoping for."

Mark added, "We didn't leave over money. And being made an associate partner might have been really appealing a couple of years ago but, frankly, I think we're past that. Don't you agree, Katie?"

"I do." Katie turned and looked me right in the eye. "Bennie, we have a vision for what an accounting firm of the future needs to look like. Harrison and Co. is a reflection of Tom's vision and doesn't line up well with what we believe we'll need to be successful going forward. Tom's definition of success is not the same as ours. It isn't just about hours and billings, the work has to be meaningful, too. Harrison and Co. will continue to do well, doing what they've always done, but we want more. I know I'm preaching to the choir when I say this. You've said it yourself: we could be doing a lot more for clients. It was so frustrating watching them struggle with issues that I know we could have helped them with. Frankly, hearing that Star Industries was leaving because we weren't proactive was the final straw for me."

Mark added, "I'm afraid you opened Pandora's Box when you took us to that Level 5 Service training. You can't un-ring that bell, Bennie."

"I hear ya'. I've had many of the same frustrations. And like you, I have a purpose-driven vision for moving the firm forward. I see us doing more advisory work than traditional work. I see us attracting higher caliber clients with a broader range of needs and getting rid of the ones we don't like and the ones that don't fit our ideal client profile.

"It won't be easy making the scope of changes I envision

for the firm, but it will be worth it. Will I run into opposition? Probably, but even Howard and Newt can see the writing on the wall. They're close enough to retirement that they aren't as invested in maintaining the status quo, especially because they won't get what they want from the firm if we continue down the same old path. I don't have high hopes for them with regard to doing advisory work, but I know they will support us as we expand our services.

"At the same time, we will be starting to transition some of their clients to others in the firm. It makes enormous sense to introduce those clients to Level 5 Service as part of the transition."

I clasped my hands together in front of me on the table. "I came here to close a sale to get you back. That was a mistake. I see that now. I'm really here asking for your help. I need you to partner with me on the re-launch of the firm. The way I see it, you can start from scratch building your own firm. You'll pick and choose the clients and projects you want, but you'll also have to spread your focus between building a practice and running a practice. That doesn't leave a lot of time for family and play time," I said and made a mental note to thank Margaret later.

"Or, come back and partner with me. Help me build the advisory practice and let Margaret and I take care of the practice management piece. Focus on the things you love without having to deal with the day-to-day crap that gets in the way."

Katie let out a big sigh and looked at Mark for some feedback.

"Bennie, we weren't prepared for the discussion to move in this direction. I think we need time to consider the implications of coming back. Won't people be pissed off at us for leaving?"

"I don't think so. They're about to have so much change thrown at them, you two are the least of their worries. Actually, bringing you both back adds some stability in all the right ways."

I sat back and put my hands back in my lap. "You two need some time to think this over. And if I were you, I would want some real assurances that things will be different going forward. Here's all I ask: would you come to the team meeting at 4 p.m. today? We're making the announcement about the transition. I'm going to lay out some broad strokes for the future and ask everyone to reconvene tomorrow at noon so we can get to work. If what you see and hear doesn't instill confidence about the future of the firm, I promise not to hound you further."

"Katie and I will discuss this, and if we're there at 4 p.m. today, you'll have your answer," Mark replied. "Whatever we decide, thanks for making us such a high priority on your first day on the job. No doubt you have a ton of pressing issues, not the least of which is losing Star Industries."

"As a matter of fact, I am meeting with Jack in the morning. I'm going to ask him to give us another chance. I plan to lay out the Level 5 Service program for him to demonstrate that we not only want to serve him better, we have a methodology to make it happen.

"And a final note, something more for you and Katie to consider. If I can pull this off, I'd like you two to take the lead on the Level 5 engagements. Katie, I know that's what you've wanted to do for a long time. This is your chance. I hope to see you guys at the meeting."

I paid the bill and left the two of them to ponder our discussion. I figured it could go either way at that point. Only time would tell.

A real decision is measured by the fact that you've taken action. If there's no action, you haven't truly decided.

Tony Robbins

A Walk in the Park

Rather than rushing back to the office, I stopped at the park by the river to gather my thoughts, jotting down some notes.

My phone buzzed. It was Anna. "Hi, honey, how's your day going?"

"Pretty intense. I just had lunch with Mark and Katie, hoping to get them to reconsider. Now I'm at our favorite spot by the river making some notes for the team meeting."

"Do you know what you're going to say?"

"I'll have Tom open up the meeting and repeat basically what he said this morning in the partner meeting. Then it will be my turn. I'll say something along these lines:

"You know big developments in the past week have had the potential to really shake things up here. Sometimes that can be a good thing, a chance to step back and evaluate where we are and where we want to take the firm in the future. Tom created a great foundation for us to build upon.

"Firms everywhere are grappling with the same issues we are. Some are in denial, and others are moving their firms forward. Without going into too much detail today, I have a vision. A vision for improving the way we interact with our clients, a vision for improving the opportunities for each of you – our team – to expand your skills and to ensure a more rewarding work experience . . . " I trailed off. "Something like that. If I'm lucky, Mark and Katie will be there, and I can talk about how I'm going to be building the firm through expanded advisory work. What do you think?"

"I think you should consider how everyone might feel if the tone of your communication is all about 'your vision.' I thought part of your vision included a more inclusive approach to building the firm," she said.

"Anna, I knew there was a reason I love you so much. You're right, of course, this can't just be my vision. Yes, I'll lead, but if the troops don't feel they have input, we won't get the buy-in and support we'll need. Thanks for grounding me. Chris said something similar to me this morning when I dropped him at school. He's a lot like you, you know."

"He's a lot like you too. He knows how much you care about the team. I think playing football and being a part of a team has really grounded *him*, no pun intended."

We both giggled at that, and Anna asked, "Will you be home for dinner?"

"Barring a mutiny, I expect to be home by 6 p.m. After dinner, I'll need quiet time tonight to prep for tomorrow."

"No problem. I'll try to keep things to a dull roar while you're working away upstairs. Love you. Got to get back to work now."

Less than a minute later I got a text from Anna: "Look inside your lunch bag when you get a chance."

And with that, I headed back to the office. I popped my head in Tom's office. He and Margaret were sorting through piles. She wasn't letting this opportunity slip away.

"Got a moment?"

Margaret headed for the door. "Stay, please. I want to check in with Tom about what he is going to say at the meeting. I think a statement from you would also be appropriate."

"Me?" Margaret seemed surprised.

"Yes, you. You're as much a part of the leadership team as any of us. Besides, everyone will be watching you for cues. We all have good working relationships with the team, but you're the closest to them. They know that you know what's important to each of them. Your blessing on this will give them the confidence to move forward."

"I think you give me far too much credit," Margaret replied.

Tom disagreed. "Margaret, I don't think you give yourself enough credit. I haven't been good about delegating, but I've never underestimated the impact you've had – and will continue to have – on the culture of this firm."

"Are we good to go?" I asked.

Tom and Margaret smiled at each other. In unison, "We're good to go."

"I'll be in my office with the door closed for a bit. See you in an hour." As I walked down the hall to my office, heads popped up here and there.

"Hi, Bennie."

"How's it going, Bennie?"

"S'up, Bennie?"

I smiled and nodded. "It's all good – See you at the meeting."

On the way back to my office, I grabbed my lunch from the

fridge, put the Do Not Disturb sign out, and settled behind my desk. Calls to return and e-mails to read, but Margaret had already handled most of them and put off what she couldn't handle until tomorrow. I opened Anna's note.

Bennie,

Remember you ARE the best man for the job. Never doubt it. The team's confidence about your leadership will come from inside you. They will follow your lead. Choose authenticity over positioning and you'll do fine.

I love you, Anna

A Door Opens

Everyone gathered in the lobby by five minutes to 4:00. We couldn't all fit in the conference room, so we frequently locked the front door and met in the open entry of the office. Some had pulled their chairs from their offices. Others were standing. I looked to Margaret for confirmation that everyone was there.

She whispered, "Howard is running late." Unbelievable, I thought.

"Are you kidding me? For this?"

Tom leaned over, having heard our discussion. "We're not waiting for him. This train is leaving the station." I was pleased to hear Tom say it.

I looked around for our special guests but saw no sign of them. I sighed, thinking about how to adjust my plan because they weren't there.

There was a knock on the front door; Mark and Katie had turned in their keys on Thursday. They'd tried the back door we usually kept unlocked during business hours but Margaret had been thorough. There was a small murmur when the door opened and they stepped through. Smiling at them, I gestured to a spot up front near me.

With a minute to spare, Howard showed up. *Amazing*, I said to myself. For once he was actually on time. I took this as a good omen for the future.

Tom threw out one of his warm smiles and began.

"Thank you for taking the time to join us today."

A couple of snickers and a comment from Jake, "Like we

had a choice?" There's a comedian in every crowd.

Tom continued. "Thanks for stating the obvious, Jake. As a matter of fact, this meeting is all about choices. The choices we make drive the outcomes we experience. You make a choice every day between staying home tucked in your warm bed or getting up and coming to work. One choice feels really good in the moment but doesn't serve you in the long run. Or maybe you chose to play gas gauge roulette because you're running late for a meeting but then you run out of gas and miss the meeting entirely. Choices shape our future, don't you agree?"

Tom was a master at turning the off-hand comment into a perfect segue.

"Everyone, *I've* made a choice. I am choosing to step down as managing partner." Before anyone could respond, he continued. "I've been an accountant for over 40 years. I started this firm 25 years ago with a vision for the firm that was consistent with the role of accountants at that time. However, as you all know, 'times, they are a-changin.' Folks, the choice I've made is the right choice at the right time. Just as the choice to have Bennie succeed me is the right choice at the right time. I am proud to announce that Bennie Stewart is your new managing partner."

There was some slight applause as everyone turned to Bennie. It felt awkward to clap as someone tells you they're stepping down. Tom made sure to ease the tension by clapping loudly and with enthusiasm. Everyone joined in, even Mark and Katie.

After a moment, Tom continued on, "Bennie has been with this firm for over 20 years. I've watched him grow as an accountant but even more relevant to his role as managing partner, I've watched him grow as a leader. He has his own vision for how to take this firm into the future. I know he has the respect of the team, and he certainly has the respect and support of the partners. I'm behind Bennie 100%. I hope you'll join me in supporting him as your new managing partner.

"Just so you all know, I am not leaving the firm – you can't get rid of me that fast. I'll be working on some special projects with the few clients I still have and cutting back on my hours over the next few months so I can spend some well-deserved quality time with my fishing rod."

Everyone laughed. Tom stepped aside making room for Margaret.

"Hello, everyone. When I was asked to say a few words today, I wasn't sure what I was going to talk about. But as I have been standing here, looking around the room at all of you, one word keeps running through my mind: family. We're a family. Scary as it is, we spend as much or more time with each other as we do with our own families. We've been present to celebrate each other's marriages and children being born, as well as supporting each other through accounting degrees, CPA exams, master's programs, and much more. We've stood by each other caring for aging parents, sick family members, illnesses of our own, and other everyday challenges.

"I joined the firm 23 years ago when you could count all of us on one hand. I remember when we merged with Newt and Howard's firm, a few years later. I remember when Bennie became a partner and when Sharon took that same step.

"I've had the privilege of working with Tom through all the growth and changes. We've had some great years, and we've had some years that we'd just as soon not remember, but through it all we've remained a family.

"I've also been present to see a lot of changes in the

profession. I can tell you this: as Tom said earlier, things are changing rapidly in the world of business and in the accounting profession. If we're to stay ahead of those changes, we all have to stick together and work as a team.

"I'm truly excited about the direction Bennie will take this firm, but he can't do it alone. The changes Bennie will propose may mean stepping out of our comfort zone a bit. Quite frankly, I'm not even sure there is such a thing as a comfort zone anymore. One man's comfort zone is another man's prison. Change can be scary, but I'm willing to embrace changes rather than run from them, because, as we learned last week, maintaining the status quo is not an option. The world will pass us by."

Some of the younger team members voiced their approval of Margaret's words with an "Amen" and "You said it!"

Margaret stepped aside and made room for me to step forward. I was touched by Tom's and Margaret's comments, but there wasn't time to enjoy them. It was now time to address the team as their leader.

"I won't lie to you. We've had a rough week. I know you all felt the shockwaves on the heels of losing two major clients and two valued team members," I said, with a nod to Mark and Katie, "in the span of a few days. Although each of these events may have seemed like they came out of the blue, they've been brewing for some time. The reasons behind these events are probably known to all of you. This is not an indictment of Tom's leadership, just bumps in the road every firm is dealing with. We could spend a lot of time dwelling on the past, but I would rather focus on the future.

"I'm sure you've all noticed that I invited Mark and Katie to be here today. I did so with the hopes of demonstrating to them and all of you that I mean business. No offense, Tom, but we haven't always been good at following through on our good intentions."

"None taken, Bennie."

"We have been so busy – with our heads down and our tails up – making sure we were doing things right, but not necessarily asking if we were doing the *right things*. I'll explain what I mean by the 'right things' later.

"For now, I want to reassure you the firm is in great shape, and you needn't worry about your future. Our conservative fiscal nature ensures we have the cash to weather the short-term storm, even after losing our two biggest clients." I looked around the room, letting the fact sink in.

"At the same time, we can't go back to operating as though nothing has happened. We've been blessed with a wake-up call that we can't and won't ignore. We've had less consequential wake-up calls in the past, when we've chosen to hit the snooze alarm. Snoozing has led us to some of the issues that, as we speak, are right up in our faces.

"Here's what I want. I'd like all of you to clear your schedules to be here from noon to 2 p.m. every day this week. Tomorrow, I'll outline the specifics of how we will move forward. If you have a conflict that can't be rearranged, see Margaret. Otherwise, I expect to see all of you on time and prepared to dive in at noon tomorrow. Lunch will be brought in each day.

"I know I can't do this on my own. Frankly, I wouldn't want to even try. I'm certain that we can – and will – get to a better outcome by working together. Any questions?"

Kristine, a brand new manager to the firm, raised her hand.

"Are Mark and Katie going to be here tomorrow?"

"I don't know, let's ask them."

I knew it wasn't fair to put them on the spot, but the cat was out of the bag. Everyone turned toward them. Katie and Mark looked at each other.

Katie asked reservedly, "Do you want us to be here?"

A chorus of affirmation followed. Jake, the comedian in the firm, said, "Does this mean I don't get your office, Mark?" Everyone laughed.

Mark addressed the group, "Thank you for that vote of support. We stepped away from the firm because our vision for the future didn't seem to be compatible with the firm's vision. We're here because Bennie asked us to give him a chance to prove that we have the same vision. We're willing to give Bennie a chance. At the same time, we want to be brutally honest that if it feels like our visions don't match up, we'll have to consider other options. We're hopeful, but it wouldn't be fair if we weren't perfectly honest with all of you."

Everyone was watching me for my reaction.

"It's my turn to be perfectly honest. If we're to have a prosperous future, we *all* have to commit to doing whatever it takes to make our vision a reality. I can't do this alone. If we succeed, we succeed together. If we fail, we fail as one. I'm willing to bet on all of you. I hope you will do the same for me.

"We're likely to hit some speed bumps in the road, but they won't derail us. Tom started today out by talking about choices. Moving the firm forward in a new direction is a choice. It's a choice we will have to revisit every day, when we get busy and shifting priorities get in the way.

It's a choice that we'll have to reinforce in each other when we get off track. Each and every one of us will have to take a leadership role in the firm to hold others accountable to the vision we set for ourselves.

"Your homework for tonight is to come back tomorrow prepared to answer this question:

"Why are you an accountant and why do you want to work in public accounting?

"Take notes as you ponder this question. You'll be sharing your answers with each other tomorrow." I glanced at Tom who gave me a slight nod. "Thank you, everyone. That's all for today. I'll be in my office for the next hour if you want to stop by with questions or concerns. Mark, Katie, may I have a moment?"

Mark and Katie followed me to my office.

"Thanks, guys, for coming. I'm sure you must still have doubts. Frankly, I do, too. But I'm starting to think we can actually pull this off. I'll talk to Margaret, but I believe the paperwork has already been processed and that you are no longer employees. For now, until you feel sure that you want to commit to the firm, we can set you up as independent contractors working for the firm on a special project. How does that sound? Harrison & Co. will be your first engagement."

"That sounds fine, Bennie. What's the special project?" Mark asked.

"Well guys, I'm hiring you to launch the Level 5 Service program. All that planning you've been doing for your own firm, setting up processes and defining your deliverables, I want you to do that for us. You'll take the lead on the Level 5 Service initiative. I know it's short notice, but I'd like you to educate the team on Level 5

Service on Wednesday. Can you be ready by then?"

"Day after tomorrow?" Katie looked at Mark, wide-eyed.

Mark had already thought it through, "It's simple Katie. We'll just go back to the Level 5 training manual and follow the directions. It's already laid out for us; we just have to tailor it to the firm."

"So you're good to go?"

"Okay, Bennie we'll do our best." Katie replied.

"That's all I can ask."

Margaret stuck her head in and coughed, "There seems to be a line forming in the hallway outside your door."

"Thanks, Margaret. Could you please set Mark and Katie up as independent contractors? They'll be consulting with the firm to launch the Level 5 program."

"Sure thing." She looked at Mark and Katie and said, "Follow me."

Over the next hour, nearly every employee stopped by, not with questions or concerns, but with congratulations and words of support. It was a bit overwhelming. I hadn't intended for it to go this way, but there were a couple of people conspicuously absent. I made a mental note to follow up with those people the next day and headed home.

It was good to get home; it had been one heck of a day. A great day.

"We're having pisgetti for dinner, Daddy!"

"Thank you, Susie, I love spaghetti. What can I do to help?"

Anna smiled, "Could you please help the girls set the table? Chris should be home from practice any minute."

"You bet. By the way, thanks for the special note today. It came at just the right time."

"You're welcome. How was the meeting? Did Mark and Katie show up?"

"Yes, they were there. I didn't really follow the script, I just spoke from my heart. Nearly every person in the firm came by my office afterwards to congratulate me and offer their support."

"Who didn't stop by?"

"Rick Carney and Mike Jones."

"Does that concern you?"

"A little, but I'll follow up with them in the morning. I'm trying not to assume anything until I know for sure what's going on with them."

After dinner, baths, and bedtime stories, I pulled out my binder from the Level 5 Service training, my journal, and random notes I'd tucked into a file called "Firm Ideas."

My outline came together pretty fast:

Why do we exist?
Are we living up to our Why?
What's missing?
What are we going to do about it?

Before I was ready to let go and get some sleep, I put together a task list. It wasn't in any particular order:
- ✓ Onion bagel with salmon cream cheese
- ✓ Venti Americano, black

✓ Notes for Marshall meeting – Level 5 graphic
✓ Follow up with Rick and Mike
✓ Review client responsibilities and start delegating projects
✓ Review Tom's To Do list to see what I need to take on or delegate to Margaret
✓ Meet with Margaret for team bios and briefs
✓ Review internal project tracking for status of work in the office
✓ Margaret – firm administrator?
✓ Set the agenda for the lunch & learn meetings
✓ Confirm Wednesday's agenda with Mark and Katie

Tuesday

I walked into Jack's office, breakfast in hand.

"Good Morning, Jack! Thanks again for taking this meeting."

"Hell, you know I can't turn down a free breakfast. Seriously, I'm curious to hear what you have to say. My conversation with Tom was long on apologies, short on a fumble recovery plan. I'm not promising this will change my mind about moving my work, but I'm listening."

Both our boys played football, and fumble recovery was the perfect metaphor, reminding me "we had dropped the ball."

"Fair enough, I appreciate that, Jack. You told Tom, but tell me what was missing in the relationship."

"Glad you didn't ask what was wrong with the work, because there was nothing wrong with the work. You guys are as good as it gets as far as accounting services go. I just feel you could have done more to help us navigate through the recession. No one from the firm picked up the phone or stopped by just to see how we were doing. Any and all conversations were limited to tax and accounting work. I was *always* the one that initiated the conversation about margins, cash flow, et cetera. In fact, we had a few months when we had to stretch out our accounts payable. The only person from the firm I heard from was Margaret, wondering when we were going to pay. Polite, of course, but it rubbed me the wrong way.

"Once, Katie was here, meeting with our controller. She offered to help us look at our cash flow and do some kind of financial stress test. Then I never heard back."

I cringed, and he saw it on my face.

Jack said, not unsympathetically, "Sometimes the truth hurts."

"That was my fault. Katie asked me about doing that project for you, but I told her to hold off. Katie's heart was in the right place, but we've been focused on the wrong things. I'm truly sorry for it.

"I appreciate that you still have confidence in our accounting services. I also agree that it isn't enough anymore. A big part of my job for the next couple years is re-tooling our people and formalizing our advisory services to respond when clients need our help."

Jack spoke emphatically, "Forgive me, but I'm calling you out on something. I don't want you to *respond* when I call, I want you to watch over things, and come to me even *before* I know there's a problem. For example, I knew my margins had been slipping for a few months, but it wasn't until our year-end tax meeting that you even brought it up. Even then, you didn't say much more than you'd noticed margins had slipped.

"Here's the point: don't tell me things I can obviously see in my own profit and loss statement, help me figure out how to fix the problem. Better yet, help me address the issue *before* it becomes a problem."

"You're right. We should be more proactive, and we will be."

"You guys always sound so smart talking about what has already happened. Any accountant can read the numbers off the statements. Hindsight is 20/20. I don't want hindsight. I want insight. I want you guys looking for the things I'm too busy to see. I want you to help me plan for the future and keep me on task, progressing toward my goals.

"My executive team regularly reviews our company dashboard – not just looking for what we need to do better. They are always trying to forecast the future performance of the company. I want some foresight, too!"

I made a mental note: hindsight – insight – foresight.

"I'm going to be really straight with you, Jack. What you're describing is foreign territory for accountants. Most of us live in a world of certainty, where everything is black or white. The minute we cross over from talking about the past to forecasting the future we enter a world of uncertainty and run the risk of crossing the line of independence. If it sounds like an excuse, I don't want it to. But it is a reality in the profession that I'm trying to deal with.

"The good news is I'm not the only managing partner with this issue on his plate. The entire profession is rethinking its role with clients for the very reasons you just talked about. Increasingly, our clients want us to act more like an outsourced CFO rather than a traditional accountant. Some would even argue that we need to be more like a CIO – a chief information officer – to offer up better business intelligence."

"That sounds great to me. What's wrong with that picture from your perspective?"

"Nothing, really, except the rules governing auditing and independence tend to make us very cautious about stepping over the line."

"Are you saying that to maintain your status as a CPA firm, you can't help me run my business? Sounds like you're working for the banks or the IRS rather than doing what's best for your clients. Remind me again, who's paying your bill?"

"True enough."

"Bennie, you're not doing such a hot job wooing me back. But you're also scaring me, because if that's what every firm is like, I'm no better off moving my business. Maybe I'm trying to buy apples from the butcher, and it just isn't going to happen."

"No, I didn't say that Jack. In fact, what I came to share with you might be just what you're looking for. A couple years ago, a few of us attended a program on how to develop and deliver advisory services that don't cross over that line. At the core of that training was what they called 'Level 5 Service.' Here, let me show you what it looks like."

I pulled out the Level 5 graphic and laid it on the table.

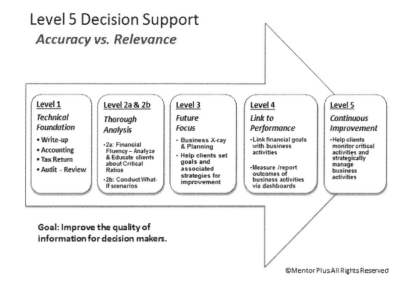

Jack scanned the document and was quick to comment, "I like it already, Bennie, especially the part about decision support and accuracy vs. relevance. To me, that kind of says it all, right there."

I dove right in, "Let's look at the levels.

Level 1 - *Technical Foundation*
- **Write-up**
- **Accounting**
- **Tax Return**
- **Audit - Review**

"Level 1 is where every accounting firm lives. It's our comfort zone. It's something we're really good at, so naturally we gravitate to it. At the same time, it's difficult to differentiate our services at that level; being good at Level 1 is an assumed competency. Level 1 is the foundation for good decision-making, because if you don't have the technical foundation right, every assumption you make thereafter is flawed.

"Once we've got Level 1 right, we can move on to Level 2.

Level 2a & 2b - *Thorough Analysis*
- **Level 2a: Financial Fluency - Analyze & Educate clients about Critical Ratios**
- **Level 2b: Conduct What If scenarios**

"Level 2 is broken into two phases. In fact, you nailed it when you talked about hindsight and insight. Level 1 is hindsight. Level 2 and beyond is where the insight and foresight kick in. Level 2a is all about financial fluency: helping clients better understand their businesses from a financial perspective. It's more than just regurgitating the numbers. It's about helping you really understand and gain insight as to what those numbers *mean*. We use the term 'fluency' because it accurately conveys what this step is all about. If you've ever traveled abroad, you know that the more fluent you are in the local language and customs, the more enriching the experience. The same is true of financial language.

"Clients shouldn't have to have their accountant play interpreter with their own financial information. Our goal is to make sure our clients can fully comprehend the implications of what shows up on their financial statements.

"Level 2b takes that financial fluency skill and allows you to do some 'what if' calculations on the most critical ratios in your business. We have a piece of software that illuminates the cause/effect between seven key business drivers and what shows up on the financial statements. We can even test assumptions of growth and cash demands or stress-test key ratios to see where you're most vulnerable."

"I'm stopping you right there. That's what Katie was talking about, right? Why you haven't shown me this before?" Jack interrupted, looking mildly annoyed.

"There are plenty of reasons but, honestly, they're mostly excuses that center on not wanting to look stupid. You see, this type of dialogue is new to most accountants. It moves us from the world of black and white, right and wrong compliance work to the ambiguity of what-ifs and unknowns."

Jack seemed genuinely frustrated. "I don't know whether to be mad at you for not showing me this sooner or to feel sorry for the accounting profession. Without something like this, there are a lot of clients like me that are going to be looking for other professionals to rely on. Do you want to be on the compliance side of things or someone I can rely on when times get tough?"

Talking to Jack was proving incredibly productive.

I made another mental note: compliance to reliance.

"That transition, from compliance to reliance, as you called it, is the journey a lot of accountants are starting to really focus on. I'd like to say our firm is at the forefront of that movement, but that would be a lie. We did the Level 5 Service training a couple years ago, came back excited about what it would mean for our clients. And yet –"

"And yet, what? Why weren't you out pounding on doors during the recession, helping small businesses figure out all this stuff?"

"We should have been. I can't fix the past, but part of the reason I'm so excited about being named managing partner is that so many of the obstacles holding us back two years ago are gone. Now, it's on me to make sure we don't drop the ball on this."

"Okay, what happens at Level 3?"

Level 3 - *Future Focus*
- **Business X-ray & Planning**
- **Help clients set goals and associated strategies for improvement**

"Think of it this way, if Level 2 addresses the accuracy piece, Level 3 sets up a context of *relevance*. At Level 3, we take you through a Business X-ray to benchmark your company's performance as compared with other successful companies of similar size. We also work with you from a strategic perspective, to understand your vision and make sure you have a clear plan for executing that vision. Borrowing from Stephen Covey, 'Beginning with the end in mind,' knowing where you want to go in the future helps us tailor information to support strategically focused decision-making. It's the difference between managing the business day-to-day and managing toward a desired outcome."

Jack was leaning forward, "Are you telling me that there are some predictable standards of business performance that you can compare my company to?"

"Yes. The Business X-ray looks at your company within the context of 7 Stages of Growth. At each of the stages, we can evaluate how your company is handling the critical issues at your current stage and predict the challenges you will face in the future. The X-ray tells us if you're ahead of or behind your growth curve, and where you need to focus your energies to be more successful. It's kind of like when you took your son to the pediatrician, and they could predict his adult height based on where he measured on the standard growth percentile. We can do the same for your business.

"Beyond the X-ray that evaluates where you are on the standard business growth percentile, we have a process for diagnosing issues, revealing underlying obstacles, and uncovering hidden opportunities that are specific to your company. Once we complete the X-ray and diagnostic process, we then help you and your management team map out your plan to address the gap between where you are today and where you want to be in the future."

"Okay, now we have a plan, then what?"

Level 4 - *Link to Performance*
- **Link financial goals with business activities**
- **Measure /report outcomes of business activities via dashboards**

"Here's where a lot of planning efforts seem to go sideways. Most companies are good at planning, but not so good at executing on their plans. Level 4 looks at the plan you come up with at Level 3 and translates the big picture goals into KPIs -- that's key performance indicators. We establish a performance measurement system to monitor the KPIs. Those KPIs are designed to support management decisions. Equally important, we're able to provide the team with strategically relevant feedback about how they are performing. We implement the feedback loop through the use of custom dashboards for team members."

I paused for a moment for Jack to jump in but he didn't. Either he was totally engrossed or I'd lost him.

"Is this making sense to you?"

"Absolutely. As soon as I finally get over being pissed off that you didn't come to me sooner, I could really get excited."

"Should I continue?"

"Of course."

"Let's do a quick re-cap:

"Level 1 is the technical foundation for precision decision-making. We have to get this part right. And not just from the IRS' perspective, but within the context of your big picture goals.

"Level 2 is all about insight and financial fluency for you and your team. Then, we do those what-ifs to uncover hidden opportunities and create direct linkages between key business drivers and financial outcomes.

"Level 3 is the relevance piece. There's this saying: People who aim at nothing, hit it with amazing accuracy. We have to have a clear vision of where you want to go and how you plan to get there. Knowing where you want to be in the future also helps us with tax planning at Level 1.

"Level 4 creates the links between behaviors and company outcomes. It's about providing line of sight performance feedback for everyone on the team via custom dashboards and departmental P&Ls.

Level 5 -*Continuous Improvement*
- **Help clients monitor critical activities and strategically manage business activities**

"Level 5 is about ongoing review of measures and outcomes. Level 5 is all about monitoring if you're on track to achieve the goals you've set for yourself. There's a lot of adjusting of the measures in the first few months of this process. Some measures are truly predictive of outcomes. Others end up not being as useful as we would like, but we often don't know this until we let the process run its course. Worse yet, dysfunctional measures can end up producing undesirable outcomes. So it's critical that we continually review the measures, the measurement process, as well as the outcomes.

"As market conditions change or your goals and strategies get adjusted, we end up developing new measures or realigning the ones we have to provide the decision support you need to run the company more effectively.

"Remember when we talked about why the profession is uncomfortable outside of black and white? This is why. There are a lot of unknowns and a learning curve to master as we fine-tune the measurement process. We're used to coming in with all the answers, being the experts. The Level 5 methodology demands that we not be the experts, but that we act as facilitators to help you and your team progress through each of the levels. It's a different role than what we're used to."

"How many of these Level 5 engagements have you done?"

"Zero. We're just getting started. When we got back from the Level 5 training, we learned Tom had cancer. I had to assume many of his responsibilities while he was out of the office for treatment. Bottom line, I dropped the ball. My mistake was not handing off the lead on launching the program. I should have let Mark, Katie, and Sharon run with it. As a result, we've continued to do what we've always done, 'random acts of consulting' that feel good in the short term but never get us any closer to a formalized consulting methodology we can roll out to all of our clients. Which is what you were asking for and, frankly, deserved.

"Now, it's two years later and one of our best clients has fired us because we didn't pay attention to his needs beyond the accounting side of things. I'm embarrassed to admit all this, but I can't pretend we did everything possible to meet your needs. I didn't want to look foolish in bringing this to you until we could do the process right. I was wrong. I should have."

"I appreciate your honesty, Bennie. I wouldn't have cared if you didn't get it perfect. We were really struggling with the recession and would have welcomed any help you could have offered, perfect or not."

"You're right. Being perfect is a dangerous and slippery slope. I've come around to valuing *'progress over perfection'* because what really matters is that we have to start somewhere."

"Start here. Start now."

My dad always said, **"Once a client says yes, shut up and stop selling."** Jack's response was the go ahead I was hoping for. I promised we would be calling him in the next couple days to set up a preliminary meeting to design the Level 5 Service engagement.

I was in a mild state of euphoria during and after the meeting with Jack. I felt like I was channeling the instructor from the Level 5 Service training. The instructor promised the class that if we just talked to our clients and walked them through the Level 5 process, step-by-step, we'd be able to validate whether or not this process was going to be a good fit for them. I have to admit that I had mentioned it a few times to clients, but I never followed through the way the instructor had advised.

Back at the office, I thought about what had just transpired.

The experience with Jack made me realize that the pursuit of our vision was secondary to the success of our clients. By aligning our vision to our clients' needs, we'd all succeed. I'd been so locked-in to the "service centric" approach, I was focused only on the deliverables we would be offering. The truth is, we could come up with any number of services to offer clients and still miss the mark. We had to start with their needs and work back from there. The Level 5 Service framework provided the roadmap to put the clients' needs at the center of our efforts.

Meeting with Mark and Katie at 11:00 a.m. would be fun. In the meantime, Margaret had organized a 15-page brief on each and every employee, including family vitals, interests/hobbies, status in the firm, recent performance reviews, and salary. It read a little like an online dating bio for each person. I glanced quickly at her write-up on Rick Carney and Mike Jones. As I suspected, Margaret had her finger on the pulse of the team.

Rick Carney had been with the firm four years and seemed to be progressing along the path of other young people. He was unmarried and an avid snow skier, despite tax season putting a major dent in that passion. Margaret's summary indicated no concerns about Rick's progress.

Mike Jones was a different story. Hired as a senior staff accountant two years ago, he clearly had performance issues. Mike's performance issues centered on being careless with details, showing up late, and leaving early, among others. In her estimation, Mike just wasn't engaged, and it showed.

I wandered down the hall to see if either of them was around. Rick saw me coming and jumped up. "Bennie, I had to head out after the meeting yesterday for a doctor's appointment, follow-up on a sprained knee. I just want to say congratulations on the step up. I'm looking forward to being on the Bennie Bus."

"Bennie Bus?"

"Yeah, that's what we're calling it. From James Collins' book, *Good to Great* where he talks about getting the wrong people off the bus and getting the right people on the bus, sitting in the right seats."

"That's a great book. Glad to hear you want to be on the Bennie Bus. We'll be loading up the bus over lunch today. I'll see you then."

The Bennie Bus. Anna would love this. I was sure she'd come up with a ton of metaphors that play off it. Mike Jones was nowhere to be found. I checked in with Margaret and found out he would not be at the lunch meeting today.

"Was I not clear? I thought I told everyone to rearrange their schedule to be here."

"Yes, you did. Mike told me that the client was insisting that they be done with the audit by Friday, so he didn't think it was right to put the client off."

"Would you please set up a meeting with Mike for me next

week? I'd like to check in with him to get a feel for whether or not he's going to want us to save him a seat on the Bennie Bus."

Margaret smiled, "You can thank Mark for that one. After you'd left, he and Katie went out for drinks with a few of the team yesterday. Word on the street is everyone is pretty excited about having Mark and Katie back on board. You did a really good thing – the right thing – getting them back."

"They're not totally back yet. I'm giving them some room to feel their way home. I want them to be fully committed before we hire them back. I have some pretty good news for them today that will help to tip the scales our way."

"Good news? Jack Marshall kind of news?"

"Yes, Margaret. Jack Marshall kind of news."

She smiled and gave me a fist pump, "Yes!"

"Shhh, don't say anything to anyone! I want the pleasure of sharing it."

"No problem, I can keep a secret."

"Thanks for the team briefs, they're exactly what I was looking for. Next, I need to sit down this afternoon and look at my client load. Do you have time to go over it with me? I need to know who's got room on their plate and who doesn't."

"I'll meet you in the conference room where we can pull up the master schedule and review the WIP."

"How's Tom coming along in his office?"

"He's pretty close to being done, just a few more file

drawers to go through. I think it's safe to tell him you don't want his office."

"Margaret, would you like to be the bearer of that news?"

She thought about it for a few seconds, then said, "No, I'll leave that up to you."

When I popped my head in Tom's office, I hardly recognized it. Surfaces were clear, shelves were organized, and there were only a couple of boxes in one corner. "Hey there, nice work."

"Now that Mark and Katie are back, I guess I'll just switch with you."

"No need, Tom, I plan to stay in my office." Tom started to object but I beat him to the punch. "I love my office. Plus, I like being closer to the troops. Easier for me to stay connected to the grapevine."

"That's nuts. What am I going to do with all this space? When I go part-time, it's going to be empty a lot of the time."

I had been waiting for the right moment to bring this up. "How about we give it to Margaret? She needs the room and a place to meet with staff without having to cram them in her small office."

Tom blinked in surprise, then smiled. "That's a bold move, Bennie, but I *like* it. A lot. She'll fuss for a bit, but she'll like it, too."

"I'll be passing off a lot of administrative work to her since I still have a pretty full client load. She's really so much more than an office manager. I think we should make her the firm administrator. What do you think?"

"I think that's brilliant, that's what I think. I should have thought of it." He gave me a sly look, and I wondered how long it would have been before he made the suggestion.

"How do you feel about switching offices with her?"

"Not a problem, I'm fine with that."

"Perfect, I'll talk to her about it right away. This means a raise, you know. Do you think any of the partners will object?"

"No, she's long overdue for the recognition *and* the raise."

"Done!" I said, thinking of Margaret as I said the word.

Good News is Good News

Mark and Katie were in the conference room waiting for me. I shared the news about Jack Marshall, explaining how I had approached the meeting.

"So, there it is: your first Level 5 engagement. Signed, sealed, delivered."

Mark asked, "Did you quote him a fee?"

"Not yet. Better we brainstorm that together. In fact, I'm thinking we use Star Industries as an ongoing case study to share with the team."

Katie spoke up, "I'd like hear how you saw our session coming together. We're ready, but we need to know how you want to roll it out."

"It's been evolving. Meeting with Jack really helped solidify my thinking."

I wrote on the white board: Why do we exist?

"Can you get us set up to show the team the Simon Sinek video? I think it will lay the foundation for our discussion. We'll put everyone's answers on sticky notes, and we'll organize them on the wall. I'll need you two to help facilitate this with me. Hopefully, everyone did their homework and is prepared to answer the questions I put to them yesterday:

"Why are you an accountant and why do you want to work in public accounting?

"After a discussion around everyone's why – we'll find common ground to hone in on."

I pulled out my note pad to review my notes before the meeting.

My focus:
How to build revenues?
How to keep clients happy?
How to keep the team happy?
Starting from scratch, what would we do differently?
Hindsight, insight, foresight
Compliance to Reliance
Why?
What's missing?
How do we close the gap?
Level 5 Service

I shared my revelations from my conversation with Jack, from how Star Industries would start to address the issue of lost revenues to the critical questions we need to address to keep clients and the team happy.

"The more I've pondered these questions, the more convinced I am that there is one answer for all of them: Level 5 Service. I hate to put all our eggs in one basket, but in this case, I think the Level 5 approach is the missing ingredient that will help us attract and retain great clients, as well as keeping top talent like you engaged and excited about being a part of our firm. My meeting with Jack Marshall and the fact that the two of you are standing here is confirmation of that."

Katie and Mark looked at each other and smiled.

Mark spoke first, "How do you want to follow up with Jack?"

"I'd like you to give him a call and set up a meeting for early next week. The three of us can meet with him and plan the engagement together. As for how we move forward, my plan today is to lead the team through the 'Why' discussion.

"Starting tomorrow I'd like you two to take the team through a Level 5 Deep Dive. A step-by-step walk-through and review of what's involved start to finish, beginning to end. Include the activities at each step, with an overview of available tools that support each step."

Mark smiled. "Katie is all over this. She's got each of the steps mapped out, so this should be pretty straightforward. We can handle this."

Asking questions will get you the performance you are after far better than dictating demands.

Dan James

Long Overdue

"Margaret, can you give me a few minutes?"

"Sure, Bennie. Come on in."

I closed the door, sat down across from her, and thought to myself, *this is going to be good for her. It's going to be really good for the firm and especially good for me. A win-win-win.*

"Okay, I've been doing some thinking and Tom is in agreement. We'd like to promote you to firm administrator. That means greater responsibilities, a larger office, and a pay raise. Frankly, this is long overdue. And given how much I'll need your help, it's the logical next step, don't you think?"

Margaret was quiet for a moment then she said, "Bennie, I'm honored that you have so much faith in my abilities, and I'm excited to take it on. You know I've been bugging Tom to let go of administrative details for a long time. I could never turn down the money, but what new office?"

"Tom's."

"No, that's not right. Tom can't be willing to move into this space."

"He was ready to move into Mark's office, then mine. You've done such a great job helping him organize, he doesn't need as much room anymore. And you *will* need the extra conference space to meet with the team, vendors, and for recruiting. Plus, many of the files you'll need are already in Tom's office."

"How much more money are we talking about?" Margaret asked.

"You tell me. Research other firm administrators' salaries, we'll do what's fair. I'm going to allocate the raise I would have received as MP to you. I'll take my bump as a bonus based on the firm's overall performance."

I waited for her to say something.

"Bennie," she said softly, "you're really walking your talk right now. I'm more excited than ever about the direction of the firm. I accept!"

"Wonderful! I need you to manage the internal workings of the firm so I can focus on building the practice with Level 5 Service. There's a ton of work to do and long hours ahead for us. Well put on some great music and dance our way through the chores. I'll make the announcement at lunch today. Are you good with that?"

"Music? Dance?"

"That's Anna's way of making chore time more fun. When everyone pulls together, even the impossible is possible."

"I know one of the first things I want to do is paint the entire office. It's been at least ten years since it was done. Maybe we can bring in some color to brighten the place up."

"I'm guessing there might be a few more long overdue items on your wish list. Put together a plan and budget. We'll review it together, then make it happen. Sound good?"

Margaret didn't answer, but she was positively glowing.

I continued. "A makeover is fitting if we're going to reinvent ourselves as a firm. Think of it as an extreme makeover like those shows on t.v. Are we all set for the lunch meeting today?"

"We are good to go." I suppressed a smile. When I started working for Tom, I started mimicking some of his speech patterns. Now, Margaret was using mine.

"Okay, I'll see you in a bit."

Lunch arrived. The smell alone ensured everyone would be on time for the meeting. Even Howard was on time. As they ate, I spoke.

"Greetings, team. Thank you for being on time. And thanks for the well wishes yesterday. I really do appreciate all your support. The purpose of our meeting today is to look at the big picture. I asked each of you to think about – and hopefully, write down – the reason *why* you're an accountant and *why* you've chosen to work in public accounting." I looked around the room for signs of panic, sure indicators someone hadn't done the homework, but everyone seemed to be comfortable.

"But before diving in, I have a couple of announcements. First, I need to tell you that Margaret Sullivan will no longer be our office manager."

There was an audible gasp in the room.

"What?"

"Are you kidding?"

Everyone turned to Margaret. Her expression gave nothing away.

"Margaret has accepted a new position as our firm administrator. She'll be taking on more responsibilities so I can stay focused on expanding the firm's skill set and service offerings beyond traditional services. Please join me in congratulating Margaret."

Cheers, whistles, and applause erupted. I was happy to see the response to her new role was even greater than the announcement about my promotion. She deserved the recognition. Margaret was a critical part of the plan to move the firm forward. She had already proven herself worthy of the team's support; I still had to prove my abilities.

"Glad you all approve. The second piece of business has to do with Star Industries. As I am sure you are all aware, we lost Star as a client last week. The good news is that I met with Jack Marshall this morning, and he is willing to give us a second chance. I learned a lot from meeting with Jack. He praised us from a tax and accounting perspective. His reason for wanting to find another firm is he felt that we weren't proactive enough during the recession. He was upset that the only time he heard from us was when he fell behind on paying our bill or we needed information from him to do his accounting and tax work. I hate to admit it but he was right about that. We were so focused on navigating our own way through the recession, we missed an opportunity to really make a difference with our clients." I paused again, letting it sink in. They needed to know this wasn't just smoke and mirrors: we needed to change.

"Jack's needs are no different from the rest of our clients. We're really lucky he's willing to let us prove that we can do better going forward. Here's what I know for sure: If we can help make Jack more successful, we can make all our clients more successful. I used to think as long as we did a good job on traditional services we'd be successful, but the recession reset client needs and expectations. Being a good accountant, even being a great one, isn't enough anymore.

"Our agenda for our four lunch sessions scheduled for this week looks like this:

"Today, we're going to talk about our *Why.*

"Wednesday, Mark and Katie will walk us through the Level 5 Service program. I know you don't really know what I mean when I say Level 5 Service. Yesterday I mentioned we had been doing things right but not necessarily doing the right things. Level 5 Service is the "right thing." By the end of this week, you'll understand it. And I predict that within a year, it will be embedded in our culture.

"Thursday, we're going to examine each department's role in launching and delivering Level 5 Service: accountants, bookkeepers, and admin. Each of us has an important role to play.

"Friday we will break off into teams to look at how to apply the Level 5 model in the firm. We'll continue to meet every Friday for the next month, over lunch, to work out any kinks in the process and share our progress.

"By the end of four weeks, I expect each department to have a clear understanding of their role in getting the Level 5 Service program up and running. Each department will develop ways to measure their progress moving toward their clearly defined goals. All of those measures will be organized into a firm-wide dashboard we will review together on a regular basis. Any questions on where we're headed this week?"

There were a few blank stares looking back at me. Then Jake, the de facto team spokesperson, asked, "Bennie, what if some of the team members aren't interested in delivering Level 5 services?

"That's an excellent question Jake. Think about it like this. Just as I don't expect everyone on the team to be an expert at everything we do, I do expect you each understand and be able to communicate to clients what those services entail. The same will be true of Level 5 Service. Not everyone will do the work, but everyone should be literate about the service and capable of identifying opportunities for others to follow up on.

"The purpose of our lunch and learn sessions is to bring everyone up to speed. A little upfront education will make the cross selling a lot easier. But before deciding you don't want to be involved in delivering Level 5 Services, you need to understand what it is. Is that fair?"

Everyone nodded yes.

We all watched the Simon Sinek Ted Talk video *How Great Leaders Inspire Action* as everyone finished lunch.

Following the video, we had open discussion around the content of the video. There were a few key statements that stood out for everyone.

- People don't buy what you do, they buy why you do it.
- We don't have to sell what we do to everyone, only to those who believe what we believe.
- If you hire people just because they can do a job, they'll work for your money. But if you hire people who believe what you believe, they'll work for you with blood and sweat and tears.
- Martin Luther King, Jr. delivered the "I have a dream" speech, not the "I have a plan" speech.
- There are leaders and there are those who lead. Leaders hold a position of authority or power. Those who lead inspire us.
- We follow those who lead not for them, but for ourselves.

"So, the question I want to ask all of you is, what do we believe? What is the 'why' that drives us? What are we passionate about?"

I asked everyone to write down their "why" on a sticky note. Katie and Mark gathered them up and placed them on the wall. There was a lot of overlap that quickly revealed some primary themes:

1) Want to help businesses succeed.
2) We love to make sense out of chaos.
3) We like to keep people from making mistakes.
4) We want to make a real, tangible difference.
5) We love to use our skills to improve other people's lives.

We then distilled these themes down even further and with a bit of massaging we came up with our why:

> *We exist to help our clients be more successful.*
> *We do it by improving the quality of*
> *information for decision makers.*
>
> *Better decision support leads to better outcomes, and*
> *when our clients are successful, we are successful.*

I couldn't have articulated it better. The team had done an amazing job of identifying our "why." I asked the group if they thought our current services were enough to measure up to our "why." We all agreed we had some work to do.

The meeting ended with a buzz. Everyone was excited, and Margaret was quick to capture the "why" on paper.

Looking at me, she said, "I can see us revising our website and collateral to reflect our new 'why.'"

I spent the afternoon reviewing my client load with Margaret. We rearranged engagements and adjusted assignments, leaving me with about half of the load I was carrying before. I realized, as we were sorting through the client list, there were a lot of engagements I should have passed on long ago. The unhealthy rationale of maintaining my book of business had gotten in the way of doing what was best for the clients and the firm. If I was to make the firm my most important client, I could no longer afford to "hoard" client work. Margaret took on the task of making the new assignments and setting up hand-off meetings.

On the way home, I realized the hand-off meetings would be the perfect opportunity to expose clients to Level 5 Service. Naturally, they would want to know why their account was being transitioned. I began to script (in my head) the dialogue for those meetings.

"Hello (insert client name). We're having this meeting because the firm is undergoing some changes, and we want to make sure you are fully informed and answer any questions you may have about them.

"The first change is that I am now managing partner of the firm. As managing partner, my role is to focus on the health and growth of the practice. One of the most important areas of growth will be advisory services. We are launching a program called Level 5 Service. As I transfer your work to (insert manager's name), I want you to know I will still be involved in making sure your work is done properly. Even more importantly, I will be evaluating our clients for Level 5 Service. Assuming your company is a good fit, we'll be sitting down to explain exactly what the service is and how it can help your business be more successful."

The script was rough and could use some refinement, but the approach was sound. In fact, my transition to managing partner was the perfect opportunity to wean clients off my involvement. I had no doubt that we could take a similar approach with any and all client transitions going forward. In fact, we could proactively *create* some of the reasons for transition as a means of introducing Level 5 Service to targeted clients.

When I got home that night, Anna was anxious to hear about the details of how the "why" meeting went. I shared the blow-by-blow with her and the kids at the dinner table.

Chris was genuinely interested in the discussion.

"Dad, our coach didn't show us that Simon Sinek video, but he did ask us to outline why football was important to our school, our community, the team, and ourselves. We all started out talking about how much we love the game, but he pushed us for more specifics about how the game could benefit others. We ended up with four key statements that went something like this:

1) Football is a sport that requires that we work as a team toward a common goal. No one player is more important than any other. Teamwork is a life skill that would help us for the rest of our lives.
2) Football is a great way to build school (and community) pride and spirit.
3) Football is a way of encouraging good sportsmanship and acting with integrity.
4) Football should be inclusive; there's room for everyone to participate in some way or another.

"That final statement got us really thinking about how we could include more of the community in the game. That discussion led to us inviting middle school kids and parents to come out for special clinics. Coach extended that idea to adding a 'football skills' challenge at the School Carnival. Remember when you came and helped us organize the 'Football Olympics' for the special needs kids? That event all started from our 'why' question."

I was impressed and told Chris, "What a great example of how getting clear on our 'why' can lead to so many other good things."

Caroline wanted to make a point too, "I have a 'why' question . . . Why do I have to clean my room every Saturday morning?"

I laughed and deferred that one to Anna, who jumped right in.

"Caroline, I think you're asking a very good why question. Maybe you can answer it all by yourself. Why do you think it's important to keep your room tidy?"

"I don't think it matters, Mom."

"Really? What happens when you can't find your homework or backpack when it's time to go to school?"

"It makes me late for school."

"Why is it important to be on time for school?"

"If I'm late, I have to stay in at recess."

"Why is recess important?"

"It's my favorite part of school."

"Let me see if I have it right, keeping your room tidy makes school more fun."

"Yes, I guess you're right."

Chris grinned and giggled at the interaction between Soc-Mom and Caroline. I got a good laugh out of it, too. It also got me thinking about the firm's *why* and how important it is to make sure every individual can relate to the benefit of living up to our *why*. If they can't relate to our firm *why*, they'll never be able to connect the dots between their actions and firm outcomes. That's what Level 5 Service is all about. Helping companies connect the dots between actions and outcomes and create "line of sight" ownership for everyone on their team. I needed to make sure we were applying the Level 5 Service concepts within the firm. My list was growing.

Vision without action is merely a dream.
Action without vision just passes the time.
Vision with action can change the world.

Joel Barker

Wednesday

The start of my third day as managing partner was a bit rough. Mike Jones, the "missing manager" from our lunch and learn series, turned in his resignation to Margaret via e-mail. He promised to finish out the audit through the end of the week and transition the project to someone else before signing off and heading on his way. All of this was apparently in response to her request to set up a meeting with me in the next week.

I asked Margaret if she'd had any indication that this was brewing, and she said she had a sense that Mike was not engaged, but he hadn't really ever complained. I met with Katie and Mark in preparation for the lunch and learn Level 5 Service sessions they were planning to teach. I asked them about Mike, and they both grew very quiet.
Finally, Katie spoke up, "Mike doesn't want to be in public accounting. He's tired of audit work and feels like the profession is boring."

I asked how long she had known about Mike's dissatisfaction. She said he had been hanging in there until he had enough audit hours to finalize his CPA designation, but showed signs of discontent almost from the start. In spite of the firm supporting him through the CPA exam prep process, he'd never wanted to stay in public accounting.

I appreciated Katie's honesty, but it made me wonder how many of our other young people were walking the same line as Mike. This dialogue made me wonder why Katie hadn't brought this issue to Tom's attention.

Which prompted an important question: Why are team members more loyal to a discontented co-worker than to the well-being of the firm? Still another addition to my list of issues to address.

Leadership is a two-way street,
Loyalty up and loyalty down.

Grace Murray Hopper

Level 5 Deep Dive

Everyone gathered for a lunch and learn a few minutes before 12 p.m. With lunch served, they settled in for Mark and Katie's Level 5 Service presentation. Mark began with a brief explanation of Level 5 Service training, what they got out of it, and what would be covered in the session.

Then it was Katie's turn. She was as animated as I'd ever seen her, excited and professional all at the same time. She'd enlarged the Level 5 Service graphic and positioned it at the front of the room. Next to it was a poster with our newly articulated "why" statement. It was pretty cool to see our "why", "how", and "what" next to each other; Simon Sinek would be proud. I was starting to feel some real momentum, the traction we needed to move the firm forward.

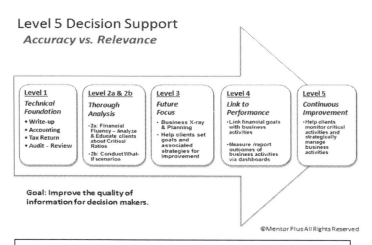

We exist to help our clients be more successful.
We do it by improving the quality of
information for decision makers.

Better decision support leads to better outcomes, and
when our clients are successful, we are successful.

Katie's presentation of the five levels was better than what I'd done with Jack Marshall. I kicked myself for not handing this over to her and Mark sooner. I realized Mark and Katie could handle the meeting with Jack without my help and felt encouraged by it. Katie outlined each level individually.

Level 1
Description: The technical foundation of sound business intelligence.
All companies need solid bookkeeping, accounting and tax services to address both the compliance and management needs of the business. At Level 1, accountants provide a foundation for a more accurate and more relevant assessment of the company's financial standing.

Ideal Outcome: Our objective is to add value to traditional services by organizing information to provide greater insight about the performance of the company by department, product, and/or services.

Associated Tools: One of the most important activities for accountants at this level is to ensure the chart of accounts is organized to provide greater management insight using a Chart of Accounts Analysis. This tool helps us improve how information is organized in the general ledger. Ideally, we can then produce custom P&Ls that can be fed into company dashboards.

Value Proposition: Through getting the numbers organized for greater management insight, we can then differentiate commodity services. It also lays a foundation for greater insight at Level 2.

Fee Potential: Hourly rate for cleaning up the chart of accounts.

Leverage: Bookkeepers, managers, and seniors can

conduct the Chart of Accounts Analysis.

Level 2a and 2b
Description: Level 2a improves our client's understanding of financial information. We refer to this as Financial and Business Fluency.

Financial statements reveal the efficacy of the business decisions made throughout the company. Typically, people think of financial statements as only important to owners and managers. In the case of Level 5 Service, we seek to raise the financial and business fluency team-wide.

Ideal Outcome: To provide every employee with line-of-sight feedback about their performance. However, feedback without a proper context and understanding does very little to advance their fluency skills. Our goal is not to simply measure the performance of the company, but to stimulate it. This requires that employees have a clear understanding of how their day-to-day behaviors impact company outcomes.

Associated Tools: Currently we use charts and graphs as a supplement to financial statements. Larger clients are provided with industry statistics as performance benchmarks. We can now go much further. The Level 5 Service program includes new tools to support our efforts:

1) Financial Fluency Presentation – this PowerPoint presentation explains fundamentals of financial statements, defines terms, and shows the link between critical business drivers and financial outcomes.

2) $COPE IT! Software provides a one page financial dashboard that gives owners and managers a new perspective on the three bottom lines in business: Net

Profit, Return on Investment, and Operating Cash flow. It answers the often-asked question, "If I made a profit, where's my cash?" The software also provides concise definitions of financial ratios using the client's own numbers. This is ideal because, as accountants, we don't always communicate how the ratios are calculated and, more importantly, what to do to improve them.

Level 2b
Description: This level takes the historical perspective provided in the financial statements and allows us to ask "what-if" questions.

What if we collect our receivables faster? How would it affect cash flow? What if we turned inventory faster? What if we held margins? Running what-if scenarios helps us identify lost opportunities and hidden assets.

Ideal Outcome: Our goal at Level 2b is to help clients think through the implications of their management decisions. We can also "stress test" the business by modeling worst-case scenarios. This helps clients cut through the issues to focus their energies on the 20% of issues that are impacting 80% of outcomes.

We can also benchmark the client's best outcomes over several years and compile them into a single scenario. This is a really powerful way of setting goals for the future based on previously achieved outcomes. The key is hitting all the best numbers simultaneously rather than haphazardly over time. And since the software is designed as a client-facing tool, clients can sit side-by-side with us and test assumptions they have about the future of their business. This lays the foundation for the planning we will do at Level 3.

Associated Tools: $COPE IT! Software is used for this step.

Value Proposition: This is one of the most important steps in the process for establishing the value of our services. If we can't quantify the lost opportunity cost of previous management decisions, we will have a much harder time establishing the ROI for our decision support services. The work done at this level helps us establish a value based pricing structure for the advisory work we provide.

Fee Potential: As a stand-alone service, the financial stress test or health check can run from $1,200- $5,000 based on the size and sophistication of the business. Multiple divisions can be evaluated individually or collectively. As part of our year-end work, we don't have to charge for this high level analysis because we see it as part of our sales process for advisory services; a few extra minutes spent with clients at year-end lays the foundation for advisory work in the following year.

Leverage: Juniors and seniors can input/import the client's numbers into $COPE IT! Software. Managers and partners can run the scenarios with the client. We'll include a high-level $COPE IT! analysis with all of our year-end planning meetings with clients. This lays the foundation for their own thinking about how they want to improve their company in the coming year.

Level 3
Description: Level 3 is about evaluating where the client's business measures up according the 7 Stages of Business Growth, helping our clients clearly articulate their vision, and plan for the future of their business.

We start with a process called the Business X-Ray. This is a series of assessments that involve the owner and management team. They are asked a number of questions that provide a snapshot about how the company is being managed, the owner's leadership style, and how they are navigating through the challenges of growth."

Katie's tone shifted from teaching to sharing, "Every year, according to the IRS, 1.5 million people start a business. They exhaust savings, borrow from friends and family, and mortgage their future to pursue their entrepreneurial dream. In five years, 800,000 of those dreams will be extinguished. I watched my dad and mom go through a business failure, and it was hard on all of us, so for me this is personal. Just imagine the impact we could have by helping our clients crack the code on business success. If my parents had been offered Level 5 Service, it would have made a huge difference."

Katie stepped back into teaching mode, "Once we've completed the X-ray, we conduct a planning session that includes a SWOT Analysis (Strengths, Weaknesses, Opportunities, and Threats) and develop an action plan that will get our clients to their desired outcome.

To ensure we maintain a balanced approach to measuring and managing the performance of the company, we use the $COPE model. Instead of just focusing on the financial performance of the company, we take a more holistic approach.

$ = Financial: This covers everything from accounting and collections to managing the financial assets of the organization. However, if we want to go beyond just measuring financial outcomes to actually improving them, we have to focus on the people and processes that drive those outcomes. We'll find these factors in the balance of the $COPE model.

C = Customers: This covers all aspects of marketing and sales, as well as ongoing customer service and retention.

Customers hold the keys to a company's success. By examining customer interactions, we can optimize and leverage every point of contact. We'll help our clients establish key performance indicators (KPIs) for monitoring and improving their cost of customer acquisition, lifetime value, attrition rates, customer satisfaction, marketing effectiveness, referrals, etc.

O = Operations: This covers everything involving the creation and delivery of products and services. We want to measure things like utilization rates, productivity, efficiency, scrap, waste, throughput, cycle time, rework, call backs, quality, etc.

P = People: No business can succeed without the right people. A clear understanding of the roles and behaviors of employees helps determine if the team is supporting the organization in achieving its objectives. We can help our clients measure things like employee engagement, training effectiveness, management development, hiring effectiveness, retention strategies, and so on.

E = End in Mind: This is where we look at the owner's business and personal goals, to make sure they're in alignment. In some cases, we might do a business valuation and some personal financial planning to make sure clients have a clearly defined path to achieving their goals.

Ideal Outcome: Our goal is to facilitate the articulation of the client's vision for their future, assess the current state of the organization, and create an action plan that closes the gap between the current state of the company and where they want to go in the future.

Beginning with the end in mind provides a context for making all our services at Level 1 more relevant. It's highly likely that we would end up adjusting the client's chart of accounts even further to provide more relevant insight based on the goals and strategy established at Level 3.

Value Proposition: Sadly, too many small businesses seldom – if ever – conduct internal planning sessions. Many even fail to hold regular management meetings. We're offering our clients the opportunity to get everyone on their management team on the same page, working on the right things, in the right way. Measuring the direct financial benefit of Level 3 may, at first, seem difficult, but establishing the cost of lost opportunities, ineffective management decisions, fragmented management structures, burnout from lack of focus, conflict from political infighting, etc., creates its own value statement.

Associated Tools: Tools available to us at this level include a complete protocol for conducting the planning session (i.e., facilitation checklists, the $COPE Diagnostic Assessment, documented processes for conducting the $COPE SWOT and Action plan steps, client workbooks, and more).

Fee Potential: Planning sessions run $2,500-$10,000 based on the size and sophistication of the business. We offer a money-back-guarantee for our services that helps to remove any resistance a client may have about venturing into this new service area with us. Some firms prefer to bundle planning into an annual retainer. Annual retainers can range from $500 to $5,000 per month.

Leverage: Much of the preparation for planning sessions can be handled by the administrative staff. A manager or partner will conduct the actual planning session with the assistance of juniors and/or seniors who will serve as scribes for the session.

Level 4
Description: Take the client's vision of the future and translate it into day-to-day activities and their associated Key Performance Indicators.

This step includes development of measures that serve as key performance indicators of progress toward the company's goals. We take a multi-perspective approach to their development including:

1) **Comparison view** – benchmarking internal and external performance metrics
2) **Customer view** – mapping the Customer Cycle of Interaction
3) **Process view** – mapping individual processes
4) **Hierarchal view** – based on the $COPE model, this is the foundation for a "balanced scorecard" approach to the measurement process

Each of these perspectives of measurement is derived from facilitated processes. In fact, the majority of Level 5 Service is about facilitating activities that engage the native wisdom of the organization. In other words, we don't go in with the answers, we ask the right questions that will help the client/team reach the answers on their own, a very Socratic approach.

If we go in with the answers, we rob the organization of the opportunity to gain the business acumen they need to improve overall performance of their organization. We want to teach our clients to fish, not give them the fish.

Once we've helped the team identify the measures that support the goals and strategy of the organization, we're ready to set up custom dashboards throughout the organization.

Ideal Outcome: Our goal is to create feedback loops providing line of sight accountability for everyone in the company. Custom dashboards limit the feedback for each level to their areas of direct stewardship.

Associated Tools: For each measurement development perspective there is a documented protocol that will guide the facilitation process.

Value Proposition: This level provides a jumping off point for raising the Strategic I.Q. (intelligence quotient) of the entire organization. We engage the team in the development of measures and, in the process, raise the business and financial fluency skills (a.k.a. business acumen) beyond the basics achieved at Level 2. The best way to define the value proposition at Level 4 is to describe what an employee *looks* like at this level:

- A strategically intelligent employee is focused on not only doing things right, but also doing the right things.
- Employees are continually looking for ways to improve company outcomes.
- Employees that understand how their behavior impacts company goals and, armed with that intelligence, are empowered to reengineer their work processes to achieve optimal performance.
- Employees know how to rearrange their priorities based on the strategic priorities of the organization.
- Employees come to work each day to grow the company, not just perform a series of tasks.

Fee Potential: Each of the facilitated modules is value priced at $1,500-$5,000 per session. The number of facilitated sessions are dependent on the scope of issues, size, and sophistication of the organization.

Leverage: Everyone can participate at this level, whether individuals are in the background developing business dashboards or out in front, leading the facilitated activities. Trained administrative staff can also play a role in helping clients establish documented processes and procedures.

Level 5
Description: Level 5 fosters an environment of continuous improvement.

Time and testing determine the ideal set of key performance indicators, which provide the most valuable and relevant insight into a company's performance. In this case, less can be more. As you can imagine, we could end up with dozens of activities to measure, but the real magic of Level 5 Service is in the refinement of those measures to ultimately settle upon a handful of critical numbers that are the true vital signs of an organization.

As market conditions change and the goals of the organization shift accordingly, the measures will shift as well. Level 5 provides an ongoing annuity for us to work with the clients. Our job is to continually ask:

- Are the numbers predictive?
- What are the numbers telling us?
- Are we on target to achieve our goals?
- If not, why not?
- Are the measures stimulating unintended consequences? Are they dysfunctional?
- What else should we be monitoring?
- What has changed in our business, market, or industry, and what does that mean to us?

Ideal Outcome: Our goal is to help the client adopt a disciplined rhythm revolving around analysis and sustained performance improvements of all aspects of their organization. We will continually cycle through all the levels in the Level 5 Service model to fine tune key activities and further develop the measurement process, over time.

Associated Tools: $COPE IT software and custom dashboards are used to evaluate company performance and provide real-time performance feedback to the team.

Value Proposition: Much like all the other levels leading up to Level 5, the value resides in the team's ability to apply their newly acquired business acumen to continually improve company outcomes. At this level, many of the lost opportunities identified at Level 2 are starting to be harvested. Owners generally observe a higher level of engagement and productivity of the entire team. They also find they can let go of the day-to-day management of operations and delegate more responsibility to the managers and team. For many owners, the greatest value to this entire process is the feeling of confidence about the sustainability of the organization and the reduction of stress associated with trying to manage everything on their own.

Fee Potential: In most cases, Level 5 Service engagements are value priced and set up on a retainer basis. The Level 5 Service approach helps us avoid scope creep through the application of facilitated modules. Because each level is clearly defined and the module protocols are well-documented deliverables, it's easy to identify activities that fall outside of the scope of the engagement and upsell those add-on services as they occur.

A typical Level 5 Service engagement could price out at a $500-$5,000 per month retainer, based on the size and sophistication of the client. The good news is this process is scalable to any size business. Likewise, the process can be deployed in any industry or type of business.

Leverage: The ongoing monthly/quarterly sessions would fall under the domain of partners and managers, with help from support staff.

Katie finished up with "That's the Level 5 Deep Dive: the highlights and the simple logic of it all."

It was Mark's turn, "Even though we have referred to ourselves as trusted business advisors all these years, we never really had any formal processes to consistently deliver on that promise. We were guilty of performing random acts of consulting and, even then, we didn't proactively reach out to help our clients. We waited for them to come to us.

"We believe the Level 5 Service model is the future of the profession. Our goal is to be ahead of the curve on this. This is a service that our clients desperately need, even if they haven't articulated it. Once Level 5 Service is explained to them, they instantly recognize it as the missing link on their path to business success. Jack Marshall of Star Industries is a good example of this. When Bennie explained the Level 5 Service model to him, Jack was quick to give us another chance."

Mark continued, "Katie walked you through what Level 5 Service looks like from a service delivery perspective. I want you to step into a client's shoes and imagine what it means to have a company that has been taken through the Level 5 process. Let's make this personal and imagine how Jack Marshall is going to respond to Level 5 Service."

"At Level 1, Jack will be able to pull more real-time business intelligence from his accounting system.

"He'll be able to review the performance of the organization as a whole and by department. This will enable him to be able to zero-in on specific issues before they become problems.

"At Level 2, Jack will enjoy the benefit of having all his managers on the same page rowing in the same direction.

"His managers will assume a greater level of personal accountability for the success of the company. Jack and his leadership team will be able to test their assumptions , using the $COPE IT! software, around growth and strategy before committing resources.

"At Level 3, Jack will have the opportunity to share his vision for the future and get everyone on the team engaged in that vision.

"He can go from dreaming about his desired future to actually having an action plan to take him there. At every step along the way in the Level 5 Service continuum, Jack will see his managers become more strategically focused and start managing toward outcomes, not just managing activities.

"At Level 4, Jack won't have to manage every detail.

"He'll be able to let go and trust that his managers and employees are not just doing things right but doing the right things. The measurement process and business dashboard will allow him to monitor the performance of the company without micromanaging.

"As the team's business acumen and strategic awareness grows, Jack's confidence in his team's ability to self-manage will remove a lot of the uncertainty and stress he is experiencing now.

"At Level 5, Jack's company will be worth a lot more because inherent in the Level 5 Service process is the clarification of goals and roles in the organization, better documented processes, less dependency on individuals, a more sophisticated management team, and valuable business intelligence for decision support.

"Operating as a Level 5 company is the difference between having a hamburger stand and owning a McDonald's franchise. The hamburger stand is people dependent. A franchise operation is system dependent.

"Michael Gerber, author of *The E Myth, Revisited* put it best, 'The key to success is to work *on* the business not *in* the business.' The Level 5 process frees Jack up to work *on* the business.

"We see Level 5 as a service continuum. Jack will see it as the path to a sustainable, strategically managed organization that he will be able sell someday for much more than it is worth in its current state."

Mark transitioned to Q & A "Do you have any questions or comments?"

Jake jumped right in, "If you went through this training two years ago, why has it taken us so long to get up and running with this? It seems to me we should have been doing this for all of our clients who were struggling with the recession."

Mark turned to me for the answer.

"Jake, that's a great question. I wish I had a more satisfying answer but I'll tell you what I told Jack Marshall. The accounting profession is very black and white. We like it when all the numbers add up at the end of the day. We don't like the ambiguity and uncertainty associated with advisory work. And mostly, we don't want to look stupid by not having all the answers.

"Because we're experts, right? That's why we have always focused on developing the technical expertise of our staff. But in every mature industry, as the accounting profession most certainly is, our ability to differentiate ourselves from other firms has become more difficult.

Why? Because every firm in the world can deliver Level 1 Service. Whereas, we used to really think of our technical skills as our differentiation, those same skills are now an assumed competency.

"It's like trying to claim that cloud computing is a competitive advantage. In a very short amount of time, all our efforts to go paperless and move to the cloud will be seen as assumed competencies. We have to be able to balance our high tech competencies with high value advisory/people skills to thrive in the future."

The joker was gone. Jake was focused and engaged. "That's fine, Bennie, but it doesn't answer my question as to why we didn't do this sooner?"

I took a deep breath, "The truth is we were complacent. We had plenty of work, and everyone was stretched to the max. We were service centric not client centric. We had a shortsighted perspective on success. In fact, we defined success based on our ability to deliver traditional services, rather than measuring our success based on the success of our clients. In short, we dropped the ball, but there's some good news in all this, 98% of firms have been similarly complacent. That means there's a lot of room for us to move the firm forward with Level 5 Service and scoop our competitors.

"Level 5 Service is the vehicle for translating our *why* into a reality.

"We could dwell on the past or start moving forward in a new direction. I vote for building a strong healthy future for our clients and the firm. I say 'we' because I need each and every one of you to embrace Level 5 Service as a critical core competency. I want it to be the foundation of our culture. We will accept and fire clients based on their readiness for Level 5 Service. We will hire and fire staff based on their ability to embrace and adopt the Level 5 mindset. Level 5 Service is the key to so much. Here are just a few of the outcomes we can expect."

Margaret jumped up to the whiteboard and started capturing.

1) Attract and retain quality clients to the firm.
2) Attract and retain quality staff to the firm.
3) Increase our revenues without significant marketing acquisition costs by cross selling Level 5 Services to existing clients.
4) Extend the lifetime value of our client relationships.
5) Blend high tech capabilities with high-touch sensibilities.
6) Reduce our dependency on compliance work to allow for a consistent year-round revenue base.
7) Provide a clear differentiation from our competitors.
8) Stimulate more client referrals.
9) Build the Harrison & Co. brand beyond traditional services.
10) Define a new performance criteria for up and coming partners in this firm.

As Margaret added to the list, we discussed each point. I was pleased to see the team had such a good grasp on what was at stake. Their questions and comments confirmed we were on the right path.

"We could keep going, but I expect you're beginning to see how important Level 5 Service is to the success of our clients and our firm. It's important for one additional reason: many years ago, my dad taught me something called 'The Rule of Seven' that has direct applicability to what we're trying to do.

"The Rule of Seven comes from the insurance industry. They did some analysis and found that the average American has 7.2 insurance policies. They studied attrition rates and found that if an agent only wrote one line of insurance for a customer, there was an 80% likelihood that client would switch brokers within two years. If the agent could write 2-3 lines of insurance, the attrition rate dropped to around 60%. If they could write four or more lines of insurance, the attrition rate dropped to less than 20%. The numbers may have changed over the years, but the concept is still valid. Let's look at the correlation between the insurance and accounting industry.

"If we're only doing a tax return for a client, are we vulnerable to our competition?"

Everyone was nodding yes. "Okay. Let's take this a step further. If we only provide a tax return and financial statements, are we vulnerable?"

Comments like "yes," "absolutely," and "for sure" came from the team.

"The truth is, as long as we stick to Level 1 services, we are vulnerable to our competition. Plus, we end up fighting to establish our value at the commodity level of the marketplace. If we add Level 2-5 services, we not only expand our client relationships, we end up fortifying our value at Level 1. The launch of Level 5 Service is as much defensive as it is an offensive move on our part."

I noticed both Newt and Howard's attention perk up at the Rule of Seven comments. Even the most traditional accountants would soon realize that advisory services actually add a measure of security for the future. So instead of shying away from this change, Howard and Newt would hopefully embrace the logic and value associated with Level 5 Service.

Howard raised his hand slightly to catch my attention. I responded, "Yes, Howard, did you want to add something?"

"I would, Bennie. You don't expect everyone in the firm to do advisory work. At the same time, you expect all of us to be conversant about what it is and identify opportunities for Mark and Katie to follow up on. Have I got that right?"

"Mostly, Howard. You have it right with one addition. Initially Katie and Mark will take the lead, but those who are interested will be given the opportunity to tag along, learn the process, and eventually run their own engagements. Those who prefer to stay in the background can still be involved with financial analysis, dashboard development, and the like." I looked at the group to gauge interest. "Raise your hand if you think you would like to be involved in delivering Level 5 Services on some level?"

I let the moment speak for itself. Every hand in the room was raised, even Newt's. Howard read the writing on the wall pretty fast.

"Bennie, I guess it's unanimous, we are going to be a Level 5 firm."

"We already are. Level 5 Service starts with a client-centric mindset. It looks like we're well on our way. I envision a day when compliance work is the by-product of an advisory focused relationship, a day when we won't be competing for work at Level 1, a day when we are known in the community as much or more for our business acumen as we are for our accounting expertise, and a day when Level 5 Service is an integral part of our DNA. Bottom line: we have a lot to look forward to."

Tom stepped forward. He'd been pretty quiet up to this point. "Team, I want you to know how proud I am of each and every one of you for keeping an open mind on this. I wouldn't have thought it was possible for us to shift gears so quickly, but I'm glad I didn't bet on us maintaining the status quo; I would have been out a lot of money."

"Tom, I'm proud of our team also. We're the only firm in town with the Level 5 Service training. That gives us a distinct advantage over our competition. Eventually the entire profession is going to head in this direction but that won't matter. By the time other firms start focusing on advisory work, we will have established ourselves as the preeminent provider.

"Mark, Katie, thank you for doing such a great job today." Everyone applauded and both Mark and Katie blushed a bit.

The lunch and learn ran over by 20 minutes, so there wasn't any more time for questions, but I encouraged people to hold them for Thursday's session where we would be talking about how we plan to roll out Level 5 Service to our clients. I also reminded them that, on Friday, we would be looking at how to apply the Level 5 approach inside the firm.

I knew I was throwing a lot at the team all at once, and I also knew, if I backed off, we might backslide to a state of complacency. I had to seize the moment and keep moving the process forward.

My follow-up conversation with Mark and Katie went well. They were genuinely pleased, as was I, at how well they had presented the Level 5 approach and said they could *feel* the tide shifting in the room.

Everything we were doing seemed on target and well worth the effort.

Even Tom stopped by my office to talk about the shift in Howard and Newt's attitude. He remarked, "Good job bringing the two of them along. They seem genuinely excited about the new direction. I thought there might be some mediation required, but it looks like the Bennie Bus is loaded up and ready to move forward.

162

"Bennie, I'm really proud of you and I know your dad would have been proud of you too."

"Thanks Tom, that means a lot coming from you."

As Tom headed out the door, I took a deep breath. I wanted to soak in the moment. Although we still had a lot of work to do, I was feeling better than I had in a very long time. Not just better, I was optimistic and excited about our future: mine, the team's, and our clients' future.

**Trust what you know;
have faith in where you go;
if there's no wind, row;
or go with the flow.**

Ed Parrish III

Fast Forward One Year

We finished Thursday's and Friday's sessions on a real high note. Everyone was energized and had a role to play. Some were focused on launching Level 5 Service to our clients, others on applying the process internally. Most importantly, every single person in the firm had been exposed to the Level 5 philosophy, and it was becoming an integral part of our culture. At last, we had a common language providing a clear focus for everyone on the team.

Mark and Katie were able to quickly get up and running with all the tools and resources included in the Level 5 Service training program. We tapped into a mastermind group of Level 5 Service focused accounting firms and accelerated our learning curve.

Jack Marshall's Level 5 engagement has been amazing. In his words, "I feel like my team is finally performing at a level where I have confidence about our future. It's been like taking our entire company through a street-smart M.B.A. program. We now have the business fundamentals and acumen to reach our full potential."

Jack paid us $5,000 a month for the first six months. We had agreed to revisit the advisory retainer at the end of six months and adjust it accordingly. I thought we would be adjusting the retainer downward but Jack wanted even more services, which led to a $7,500 retainer indefinitely. Since launching the Level 5 engagement, Jack has referred three new clients to the firm. The nice thing about the referrals is the new clients came through the door *asking* for Level 5 Service. Jack did all the selling for us.

The lost Hallstrom, Inc., revenue was replaced in the first four months.

After a month of working on Level 5 engagements, Katie and Mark invited me to lunch to ask for their old jobs back. I'm happy to report both will be admitted into the partnership by the end of the year.

While Mark and Katie were busy running the Level 5 Service program for our clients, Margaret and I were applying the process internally.

Margaret has relieved me of 80% of the administrative duties, and she hired a new assistant who effectively replaced her as the office manager. Similarly, Sharon stepped up big time. She took up a lot of my client load initially, but then quickly developed some of our younger managers and transitioned much of it to them. She grew the team's competencies by conducting bi-weekly "skills and drills" on how to read between the lines of a financial statement. She enjoyed drilling the team on managerial accounting concepts. She would say, "I'm training my replacements so they can pay for my retirement." Sharon took full advantage of all tools and processes that were included in the Level 5 Service training. She was adamant, "No more random acts of training either!"

I'll be honest and admit we lost focus at times throughout the process. Deadlines and tax season distracted us, but we continued meeting monthly – even during tax season – to maintain the momentum. Interestingly, it was the team that really drove the momentum. They wouldn't let go of the process once they had a taste for it.

We established a Level 5 Service billing code series to

monitor our efforts and quantify the outcomes. Following our own Firm X-ray and Level 3 planning session, we established a firm wide dashboard to track some of our most critical key performance indicators like employee morale, client satisfaction, Level 5 Service revenues generated, client referrals, re-work, etc. Additionally, we instituted a state-of-the-art project tracking system that has allowed us to eliminate timesheets for most of our engagements.

We also implemented a no-surprise billing policy that requires a client conversation whenever an engagement extends beyond the agreed upon scope of services. No more scope creep! This led to our being more effective at detailing the scope of an engagement *before* it commenced. The no-surprise policy was as good for us as it was for clients. It helped us optimize our engagements and eliminate many of the write-downs we had experienced in the past.

Next, we started actively recruiting talent from the local colleges and found our Level 5 Service presentations attracted the best of the best. Jake turned out to be an amazing recruiter. One of our core strategies that came from our Level 3 planning process was to build the talent from the ground up rather than trying to teach old dogs new tricks. We found we could accelerate the teams' professional development via Level 5 Service, enabling Next Gen accountants to advance along the partner track faster than any other firm in town.

Harrison & Co. quickly became the firm of choice for new grads.

I instituted a policy of firing our bottom 10% of clients

each year to create capacity for the new referrals that keep coming through the door. We established a client review committee to evaluate prospects, and the committee routinely turns down any prospective client that doesn't look like a good fit for Level 5 Service.

Initially, there was a little push back on the committee concept because the old paradigm of any business is good business still existed. By making it a committee decision rather than leaving it to any one individual, we've been able to establish a sustainable standard for client acceptance. Word on the street is that there is a waiting list to get into Harrison & Co. It's not yet the case, but I kind of like the mystique of a "referral only" practice.

As the reputation of Level 5 Service has grown in our community, a venture capital (VC) firm approached us about establishing a Level 5 incubator program for their start-ups.

The VCs love the Level 5 model because it addresses the weak financial and business management skills of their start-up entrepreneurs. Likewise, several bankers have begun to refer clients to us specifically for Level 5 Service.

Tom retired within three months of my taking over as managing partner. At first, I took it as a sign that he wasn't comfortable with the direction the firm was moving, but he was quick to let me know that it wasn't anything we were doing it was that his cancer had resurfaced. He was able to battle it and is hanging in there. Connie insisted that he quit working and devote his time to loving her, fishing, and grandparenthood, in that order, and he did.

He likes to tease me by sending photos of his latest catch.

Tom was an important part of my life for over 20 years. Today, I miss Tom almost as much as I miss my dad. I've thought about my dad a lot in the past year. There have been long hours trying to balance client and firm responsibilities, not to mention family. There were many days when I questioned my sanity for pushing the Level 5 Service model so hard. It would have been much easier just to replace a few lost clients, hire some more talent, and maintain the status quo. Whenever I felt overwhelmed or lost, I would just ask myself, "What would dad do?"

I often felt like my dad was right beside me, encouraging me, cheering me on. I'm glad I didn't deviate from the vision. I've been to a few conferences over the last year and heard other managing partners share their grief and frustration over trying to move their firms forward without a clear destination in mind. The resistance to change plaguing the profession has paralyzed them. Over beers at one of the conferences, I joked that if they really want to shake things up, they should fire their two biggest clients and two of their top managers. They looked at me like I was crazy.

I'm amazed at what we've accomplished in one year.

I honestly didn't think it was possible when we started, but as it turns out, the starving crowd was a lot hungrier than we realized and making the transition from compliance to reliance via Level 5 Service was not nearly as difficult as we feared it would be. Once the team got a taste of Level 5 success, they were more willing to put in the hours to expand their skills and get the work out the door. Even Mike Jones, who had given notice, reconsidered his exodus from the profession when he got back to the office and heard about the changes that were already underway. As committed as he said he was to the profession, his behavior didn't match up with his words and, in the end, we let him go after a couple months.

Margaret has set the bar pretty high for new hires, instituting a number of new assessments into the interview process that measure "people skills" in addition to technical skills. As she puts it, you can teach people how to do the work, but if they lack the emotional intelligence to connect with clients on a personal level, they won't fit in with our client-centric culture. She's always polite when she encourages unsuitable candidates to interview with our competitors. Amazingly, our competitors have thanked us for the referrals. One man's trash is another man's treasure.

Gotta love that Margaret; her strategy pretty much guarantees that we're the *go to* firm in town for forward thinking entrepreneurs.

As I cleared off my desk this afternoon, I was struck by the fact that there I was, still sitting at the same desk in the same office as I had been a year ago. So much was the same in spite of how much things had changed. Margaret had seen to it that the entire office had a facelift including painting my office. She even tried to update my furniture, but I turned that down, happy with my office just as it is. Although, the painting project gave her the same opportunity to help me clean out my office as she had for Tom.

I like my office being close to the team. I even grew to appreciate having to walk across the office to talk with Margaret.

It makes me more visible and accessible to the team.

Sometimes it's the journey that teaches you

a lot about your destination.

Drake

Champagne, anyone?

I walked into our house at my usual time late afternoon on Friday to hear, "Surprise!"

Anna and the kids were there. Nomi, Carl, Karen, and Josh, along with their boys, all jumped out from various hiding places. I was a bit confused because Anna had me expecting a little dinner party for Karen's birthday. It was a ruse to distract me. Today was, in fact a year to the day when that Moment of Truth forever changed the trajectory of our firm, our clients, and my life.

Josh popped the cork on the fancy champagne – the good stuff this time – while Carl and Nomi had great fun making a similar fuss over the sparkling cider for the kids. With glass in hand, Josh led the toast.

"Here's to Bennie our trailblazer! May he continue to shake things up! We're all really proud of you, Bennie."

I felt everyone else deserved the toast. I couldn't have stayed focused on the firm without the help of the family, so sharing this moment with them was particularly sweet. Carl and Nomi deserved a toast for stepping up with the kids. They had tag teamed on childcare duties and supported Anna and I as we tried to juggle our busy schedules.

Looking across the room, Carl and my mom seemed to be enjoying a private champagne toast all on their own. It reminded me of one of those parent-to-parent glances, catching each other's eye and sharing a joyful moment over something your kids have accomplished. Or, perhaps they were toasting to something much more personal. I wouldn't exactly call it a romance, but there is definitely a sweet devotion to each other that didn't exist a year ago.

Josh pulled me aside to tell me how thrilled he was with what he was getting out of Level 5 Service. His company had already been successful, but he'd volunteered to be one of our Level 5 guinea pigs. Much to his surprise and delight, Mark and Katie had been able to refine his key performance indicators and improve his business intelligence beyond what his trusted business advisor, Paul Henry had done. Imagine that.

"I take back all the things I said to you last year," he began. "I have a whole new respect for you and what you've accomplished. I was with my CEO Forum last week, and the subject of CPAs came up. It was a perfect opportunity for me to toot your horn. And I did, telling them I could honestly say your firm had surpassed my expectations, and I could now call you my most trusted business advisors and mean it. Don't be surprised if you hear from some of them about Level 5 Service, especially the Business X-ray part. They were *very* interested."

After everyone had left and we'd put the house back together, Anna and I headed out to the patio to enjoy the quiet.

Leaning on my shoulder, Anna said, "Well, Bennett, you've come a long way since we sat out here a year ago contemplating the future of the firm and your future as its leader. You must be feeling pretty proud."

"I couldn't have done it without help from a lot of people, no one more than you, my love. You kept me focused and believing in myself when I questioned my sanity for jumping into the deep end of the pool."

Anna responded, "Over the years, I've seen you work fewer hours and come home exhausted and unfulfilled. This past year, I watched you work harder than ever and yet you've had more fun than ever. You're happier than you've been since college. You were never miserable, but I know you kept on working hard even when you weren't feeling very fulfilled. As a good provider, father, and husband, it's your way, but it warms my heart, seeing the spring in your step and sparkle in your eyes. Even nights when you'd come through the door with hours of work under your arm, you weren't beaten up and worn down like before."

"*You*, Anna, got the Bennie train moving again, suggesting we re-launch the firm starting with 'why' we exist. It's the foundation for all we do. It's been a compass to put us back on track when we might have strayed off course. By the way, Margaret ordered new business cards." Anna hadn't seen them. I pulled one out and handed it to her.

On the front side it read:

Harrison & Co. Accountancy, LLP

Bennie Stewart

Level 5 Service Champion - Fearless Leader

bennie@harrisonco.com
www.harrisonco.com
Ph: 831-659-7587

Accepting clients by referral only.

On the backside it read:

We exist to help our clients be more successful. We do it by improving the quality of information they have to make decisions.

Better decision support leads to better outcomes, and when our clients are successful, we are successful.

Anna carefully read both sides of the card. "I guess that says it all, doesn't it?"

"It sure does." And with that we finished the last of the champagne and called it a day.

The end or maybe just the beginning . . .

Are you ready to move your firm forward?

Afterword

Although Bennie's story may not be exactly like yours, the motivation for wanting to make a difference is probably the same. Like all of us, Bennie wants to know that what he does matters. If you already have a passion for helping others, the Level 5 Service model has the potential to transform your passion into something tangible and meaningful for the clients you serve as well their employees and customers.

Hundreds of thousands of businesses fail every year (millions worldwide). I'm not saying we should be on a mission to eliminate all business failures; the beauty of a free market ensures the best outshine and outwit the poor performers, resulting in a healthier economy for all. On the other hand, there are a lot of small businesses that perpetually straddle the fence between surviving and thriving.

I figured out a long time ago that there are three kinds of businesses:
1. Throw-ups = undesirable
2. Start-ups = unproven
3. Set-ups = under-developed

Throw-ups deserve to fail, clearing the way for their competition to shine. Whether it's the arrogance of an owner, a poorly conceived business model, or a lack of focus/energy, don't waste your time. Move on.

Start-ups still have to prove they have a viable product or service and there is a market that wants it.

Set-ups comprise the vast majority of small businesses. They have a proven product/service already validated by customer sales and yet they still struggle. The struggle comes from not having a good grasp of business fundamentals. To move a struggling set-up to a level of sustainable performance there are three degrees of effort:

1. Tweak: clean up inefficiencies, fine tune business intelligence.
2. Tune-up: systems focus, eliminate tribal knowledge, focus on management team development.
3. Overhaul: re-launch, streamline deliverables, messaging, business model, and the punch list goes on.

The Level 5 Service framework allows for the scaling of services based on the breadth and depth of issues your clients face.

I'm often asked why an advisory framework like Level 5 Service so critical. Here's why. I occasionally meet practitioners who are already doing a lot of advisory work with their clients – generally very good work. If you are one of those advisory "savants" who has successfully combined years of experience and your natural consultative abilities into a successful consulting practice, congratulations! If you like being a lone wolf and are comfortable building a practice that is totally dependent on your skills, I wish you every success.

On the other hand, if your goal is to build a firm of trusted business advisors, having a step-by-step advisory protocol that everyone can follow is the only way to go. You wouldn't dream of running a tax or accounting practice without systems for producing and documenting the work. And yet, firms allow their highest value advisory work to be performed without the same kind of systems and/or quality controls.

A framework, system, process, protocol (whatever you want to call it) is the only way you can institutionalize quality service across the firm. If you already have an advisory protocol that is working for you, I hope you were able to extract some ideas from this book that will serve to enhance your current approach. If you don't already have a systematic approach for advisory work, I hope you will give the Level 5 Service model a test drive.

Test Drive Level 5 with Five Clients

Present the Level 5 Service model to five clients. Go to the resource section to learn how/where to download your own copy of the model. Use the language and scripting Bennie used with Jack Marshall when you present it to your clients and/or prospects. Watch for a reaction. You'll know almost immediately if they are a good fit for Level 5 Service. If the first client you show the model to doesn't bite, don't give up. Keep going. Based on feedback from hundreds of accountants who have gone before you, I can almost guarantee that at least one (and probably three out of five) clients/prospects will indicate some level of interest. If you really want to have some fun, introduce prospects to the Level 5 Service model and watch your close rate go up.

If Bennie's story didn't convince you the Level 5 Service model is the right way to go, perhaps your clients' and prospects' reaction will.

*Where performance is measured, performance
improves. Where performance
is measured and reported,
the rate of improvement accelerates.*

Thomas S. Monson

Resources

Throughout the book, there are references to authors, tools, and programs that deserve more explanation. There are also a great many books and links that wouldn't fit in the story but deserve mentioning.

Recommended Reading:

Book - Resource	Author - Link*
Escape Velocity: Free Your Company's Future From the Pull of the Past	Dr. Geoffrey Moore
Crossing the Chasm	Dr. Geoffrey Moore
Transforming Client Services: A White Paper	Dr. Geoffrey Moore Available for download at www.cpa.com
Navigating the Growth Curve: 9 Fundamentals that Build a Profit-Driven, People-Centered, Growth-Smart Company	James Fischer You can download his book at www.growthcurveinstitute.com
Leadership Simple	Steve Morris & Jill Morris
Three Signs of a Miserable Job Getting Naked Silos, Politics, and Turf Wars Five Dysfunctions of a Team	Patrick Lencioni
Raving Fans – A Revolutionary Approach to Customer Service	Ken Blanchard, Sheldon Bowles and Harvey Mackay

Book -- Resource	Author - Link*
Emotional Intelligence	Daniel Goleman
Good to Great	James Collins
Built to Last	James Collins
Open Book Management; The Coming Business Revolution	John Case
The Great Game of Business, Updated	Jack Stack
Managing By the Numbers	Chuck Kremer, John Case, Ron Rizzuto
Inc. Magazine	Search on performance measurement, critical numbers, key performance indicators
Implementing Value Pricing: A Radical Business Model for Professional Firms.	Ronald J. Baker
Extraordinary Guarantees: A New Way to Build Quality Throughout Your Company & Ensure Satisfaction for Your Customers	Christopher W. L. Hart
The Abraham Group	There are a number of free resources by Jay Abraham @ www.abraham.com
Level 5 Test Drive Kit	www.myfirmforward.com

In addition to all the great books and resources on the list above, you can find a number of articles, white papers, and other resources at www.mentorplus.com

I'd love to hear from you! Feel free to send me an e-mail and let me know how your Level 5 Test Drive worked out.

All my best,

Edi Osborne

Contact info:
Mentor Plus
P.O. Box 389
Carmel Valley, CA 93924
Ph: 831-659 PLUS (7587)
edi@mentorplus.com

Go to www.myfirmforward.com

to access the Level 5 Test Drive Kit

About the author:

Edi Osborne is a recognized expert in the development and delivery of performance measurement and management services. CPA Practice Magazine has named Edi as one of the Top 25 Thought Leaders and Most Powerful Women in the accounting profession. She is co-author of *Driving Your Company's Value* published by Wiley.

She is co-founder of the Mentor Plus® Consulting Accountants Round Table, author of the Mentor Plus® M.B.A. - More Business Acumen Program and Certification in Strategic Performance Management (CSPM).

She is certified and fluent in a number of behavioral assessments including DISC, Motivators, Emotional Intelligence, and Tri-metrix Talent Management System.

As a business intuitive, Edi has helped many individual practitioners and firms address obstacles to growth and reach new heights. Her entertaining and down-to-earth style makes her a favorite speaker at conferences, effective facilitator for firm retreats, and transformational coach to aspiring leaders.

44016771R10105

Made in the USA
Charleston, SC
15 July 2015